'While anxiety can burn some calories, it ain't good for you. In *Up Yours!* Mark Butler shares a real, accessible, funny, and actionable guide to generate more care, compassion and balance for oneself and others in our overly fast-paced world. A highly recommended read for any individual or team leader who wants to overcome burnout and thrive.'

Stephen 'Shed' Shedletzky

Speaker and author of *Speak-Up Culture*

'Mark's somewhat irreverent title sets the reader up to expect a lighter touch on what is a weighty topic with a big message – it's going to take "lifelong pursuit" not a quick fix to get on top of burnout. And that lighter touch and humour breathes life and inspiration into *Up Yours!*, as Mark maps out what burnout is and what you can do to recover from it. I especially like Chapter 11's focus on boundary setting: Mark's advice is invaluable!'

Dr Karen Morley MPsych GAICD MAPS

'*Up Yours!* codifies the response necessary for those experiencing burnout and anyone looking to protect themselves from what can be an overwhelming world. Radical self-care is the answer to our current and future environment. Organisations and individuals should take note; without these lessons we fail to thrive. Mark provides the answers we need to manage ourselves for true well-being.'

Dr Amy Silver, author of *The Loudest Guest: How to change and control your relationship with fear*

'At a time when we are all under constant pressure, with distractions, overwhelm and reactivity, being able to take control of our self-care can seem like a mean feat. *Up Yours!* keeps it simple and provides a straightforward approach you can implement immediately and see a shift in a short period. I'll be recommending this book to all my clients to get through the times ahead.'

Jane Anderson, Strategic communications expert

'Mark Butler's gem of a book, *Up Yours!*, is a practical handbook for upping your self care. Based on brain science and extensive research, Mark offers easy ways for us to take holistic control of our health. If you want simple ways to manage stress and recalibrate, this is the book for you.'

Zoë Routh, Leadership futurist and award-winning author

Up Yours!

UP YOURS!

The Pursuit of Radical Self-Care

Mark Butler

MAddBeh MGestTher CreC MPACFA (Clin)

Published by Mark Butler

First published in 2022 in Sydney, Australia

www.markbutler.com.au

Edited by Jenny Magee

Typeset by BookPOD

ISBN: 978-0-6456724-0-4 (paperback)

ISBN: 978-0-6456724-1-1 (ebook)

A catalogue record for this book is available from the National Library of Australia

This book uses stories to enforce the meaning behind its relevant chapter. Permission to use these stories has been provided.

Every effort has been made to trace (and seek permission for the use of) the original source of material used within this book. Where the attempt has been unsuccessful, the publisher would be pleased to hear from the author or publisher to rectify any omission.

Dedication

To Mary McEvilly Butler, my beloved wife, best friend, confidante, greatest supporter, constant source of inspiration, motivation and tenacity, guide, advisor and safety net.

This might sound like an Oscars speech, and I don't mean it to, but there are swathes of people I want to thank the bejaysus out of for getting me this far. I am acutely aware that by naming names, I may stuff it up and forget someone, but here goes.

A great many people have mentored me on this thought leadership journey. The highest accolade must go to Mary Butler, my dear sister, whose patience and sanity were sorely tested but who tenaciously guided me (and continues to do so) anyway. Matt Church, Lisa O'Neill and Col Fink for their brilliance, wisdom and mentorship. Also, Alex Hagan, Dr Richard Hodge, Dr Amy Silver, Colin D Ellis, Paul Matthews, Sophie Krantz, Monique Richardson, Katie Rees, Jade Lee, Shane Williams, and so many others continue to inspire and lift me every day.

In my clinical career, I have met so many inspiring individuals battling with their demons and dealing bravely with what life has thrown at them. They say that everyone you meet has something to teach you, and I believe that is so. What I have learned about grace, strength, humility, compassion, vulnerability, courage and forgiveness shapes what I do every day.

I deliberately do not name clinical clients for obvious reasons, and this habit stays with me in my work with organisations and leaders. I love my work and those I work with, and strive to go above and beyond for all of you. You know who you are – thank you for the privilege of sharing the journey with you.

This book would not have seen the light of day were it not for Jenny Magee, my patient and wise editor, and Kelly Irving, my book coach, for corralling me in the beginning and giving me structure. Finally, I thank my work colleagues, Maricon and Pablo, for their support and diligence in helping me in all that I do.

Contents

Introduction

'Life is a grindstone, and whether it grinds you down or polishes you up is for you and you alone to decide.'

— Cavett Robert

Are you wondering how to live a more balanced, fulfilling life with a revitalised view of what is important to you? How can you up your self-care to live each day with a sense of gratitude, abundance and vitality?

How can you (almost) have your cake and eat it too?

I don't just mean exercising more or changing your eating habits. I mean through greater awareness of yourself. Figure out what matters to you and how to get and keep it. Learn how to determine and declare your boundaries for self-care and get your needs met. Accept that life can be shit at times. Understand when you need to cut yourself some slack.

And most importantly, know that you are not alone.

It's a radical idea in a time of quick fixes. And it's a lifelong pursuit, not an overnight transformation.

This book is the culmination of my years of experience in clinical and corporate work with people at the end of their ropes, often succumbing to self-destructive behaviours from trying to cope with lives of overwhelming stress, trauma, neglect and abuse. Hard and often cruel times.

I was the ambulance at the bottom of the cliff.

That work was at the sharp end of what so many people experience. I was the ambulance at the bottom of the cliff, yet I knew there was so much we could do at the top of the cliff to prevent these outcomes.

We all, to some degree, face challenges that we don't deal with well. Our responses are often the result of learned behaviours or coping styles that serve us well for a while — and then don't.

In my clinical work, I have found that the only comprehensive way to treat people is through a holistic, whole-of-person approach to recovering full health. Treating or suppressing symptoms does not deliver lasting results, as we are just papering over the cracks.

The path is experience, connection and belonging. It involves growing self-awareness of what is happening from moment to moment and how we respond to those circumstances. To be at our best and most resilient takes self-compassion and self-care.

This book, *Up Yours!*, is about radically upping your self-care game. It was born from a deep need to improve how we look after ourselves and give ourselves a break in the face of increasing levels of overwhelm, burnout and exhaustion in workplaces.

It's a response to what I've seen in my clients since the Covid-19 pandemic began.

Something has shifted — something greater than we've seen since the Industrial Revolution in the latter part of the 18th century.

Before Covid, we had routines. Work-related habitual lifestyles of going to work, doing what was needed, coming home and doing it all again tomorrow. Rinse and repeat.

Almost overnight, we switched to something utterly alien to most of us, isolating and working from home. Exercise routines dropped away or changed dramatically, and the boundaries between work and home became blurred. We learned to play the banjo or to bake sourdough bread. We started to drink more, but we stopped playing the pokies. We embarked on home-schooling our kids with greater or lesser success. (Teachers reported children returning to school with a refreshed vocabulary of swear words. Secretly that delights me on some level, as I love a good swear now and then!)

Life changed dramatically. But something else seemed to shift as isolation and lockdowns dragged on. Our priorities shifted. What we once took for granted became new priorities we never wanted to lose.

On the upside, these included spending more time with loved ones and family. Being more involved in our kids' lives. Making time for things that interested us. Never feeling lonely.

On the downside, we recognised that the work commute has almost no positive or upside. But we were so used to leaving home at a particular time that we replaced the commute with work. Usually from some misguided notion that it was our boss's time, not ours. (We'll talk more about that later.)

This enlightening time showed that our old habitual routines weren't our only options. There were so many opportunities to glean more from our lives.

The pendulum has started to swing back with staged return-to-work policies and hybrid working arrangements. The Great Resignation has seen many people change roles and workplaces to find others that better meet their needs.

Organisations have begun to see mental health in the workplace as a need-to-have conversation rather than nice-to-have. Caring for employees needs to be a top priority. Their people certainly think so.

> *Self-care is no longer taking a back seat.*

As you have picked up this book, I suspect you are like millions of like-minded people worldwide. Your newfound outlook on self-care is no longer taking a back seat to anyone else's schedule or priority.

If you are reading this book, you likely want to embark on a self-care routine to improve your lifestyle, increase your self-awareness and develop a deeper level of self-compassion.

But where to begin such a pursuit? There are loads of self-care books and websites that focus on various aspects of health and wellbeing. But in my experience, you can't service your car's engine and assume the brakes and tyres will take care of themselves.

So, I will not tell you to eat your vegetables, but we *will* explore why we need to eat properly. I will not tell you to hit the gym six days a week, but we *will* explore tiny habit changes that can lead to a new and improved you.

This book is less about *what* to do and more about *why* we need to do it. You are far more likely to buy into an uplifting lifestyle if you know why you are doing so. In his best-selling book[1] and subsequent TED talk[2], Simon Sinek makes perfect sense about starting with why.

So, this book is all about you and your reasons for change.

We tend to deal with issues after they arise, rather than predicting or proactively anticipating challenges and taking steps to prevent them.

Self-care and preventative health are within our grasp.

This book is in three parts.

Figure 1: Balance model

Part One: Look Up is taking stock of how we currently behave and what influences our behaviour. These are the basics of sleep, diet, exercise and mindset. In short, if the engine isn't running well, we aren't going anywhere on our journey.

Part Two: Look In involves focusing on the areas that support our inner selves. This includes meditation, relaxation, play (a hugely important lost art), centring and grounding ourselves.

Part Three: Look Out is where we explore the absolute necessity of relationships with others, our sense of belonging and connecting, boundaries and how to ensure they are met.

Throughout the book, you will see a series of questions at the beginning or end of each chapter. I encourage you to consider the questions that are relevant to you. Share them with your partner, colleague, or friend and ask them to answer the questions honestly and truthfully about you. You may well find that they have a different answer to yours.

The process of self-awareness, self-compassion and self-care is about finding your deepest, uplifting immersion in life. The happy coincidence is that you will also find yourself healthier, more engaged and more satisfied at work. We spend so much time in a work environment (whether at home or a place of work), so why not enjoy it?

Throughout the book, I have shared an action plan that you can download as a PDF and print off (and share with friends if you like). It is an integral part of this book because it will connect to at least one task from each chapter to improve your level of self-care.

By the end of the book, you will have systematically improved your levels of self-care, integrating new patterns and behaviours across every domain of your life.

So, come with me as I offer you a wide range of small changes that will lift your game and move you towards sustainable high-performance.

PART ONE

LOOK UP

CHAPTER ONE

The Engine Room

'I'm giving her all she's got, Captain! She cannae take anymore.'

— Montgomery Scott, Star Trek Enterprise (2251)

Questions: Do you work from home, at least sometimes? Do you find it hard to switch off? When your engine isn't running properly, does it feel like you aren't getting anywhere?

In the early 1990s, I volunteered with the fire crews at Amaroo Park Raceway in western Sydney and the Mount Panorama Motor Racing Circuit for the Bathurst 12-hour and 1000 events. It was great fun with a great bunch of people, and I loved being among the action. It wasn't quite the Starship Enterprise, but fun nonetheless! And it was almost as dangerous to travel in the back of a Mazda (or any other Japanese make) fire truck, ducking full VB cans fired by Holden or Ford spectators!

It always struck me that, on the track, these touring cars could burn through an engine in 1,000 km, yet when driven as taxis, they could last 500,000 km or more. (Of course, tuning and racing performance have a bearing, but stay with the analogy for a minute).

I figured that constantly running on the red line would destroy any engine. It wasn't the engine's fault; any engine is susceptible to failure if continually placed under stress and pressure to perform at maximum capacity for long enough.

> *We fail and collapse if we run the red line for too long.*

We are the same. We fail and collapse if we run the red line for too long. Every lightbulb will blow, and every hard drive will fail if used for long enough.

It isn't enough to pour oil into the engine and expect the rest of the vehicle to operate flawlessly. Sadly, we often take better care of our cars than of ourselves. We insure them and service them at regular intervals. We know the various levels and tyre pressures they require to function correctly. We wash, wax and vacuum them.

In the same way, it is vitally important to focus on all aspects of self-care because we need a balance between the physical, mental, emotional and spiritual areas of our lives. And by spiritual, I mean more tranquillity and inner peace. We must find our balance in all these areas to maintain a healthy lifestyle. We are hard-wired to do so.

As a recent example, the Covid response has seen many of us working from home at least some of the time (when not in lockdown) or in a remote working situation.

In doing so, people are finding it hard to switch off. The concept is FOLO — Fear of Logging Off, and it's a close cousin of FOMO — Fear of Missing Out. FOLO is happening to people who are unused to working from home. They discover that they cannot switch off in the evenings, or there is a blurred line between when starting and finishing work. It can feel like we live at work rather than work from home.

We often start our workday at the time when we used to commute, which means we are working as much as an hour extra per day, or sometimes even more. Even conservatively, that could mean an additional four hours per week or eight in a fortnight; that's an extra day each fortnight. Two days extra per month. Assuming a five-day week, that's equivalent to working an extra month a year. I'm not saying we shouldn't do it, but I am saying that we need to balance that with other areas of life to ensure that it isn't overwhelming.

> *'Busy is the new stupid'*

Warren Buffet, American business magnate, investor and philanthropist, says, 'Busy is the new stupid'.[1] That may sound a little aggressive, but I agree that we need to get past seeing busy as a badge of honour. And we need to call it out when we see it.

Traditionally, being busy was seen as a sign of commitment, dedication, or passion. But now we need to work smarter, not harder. That means considering more than one element of our self-care. I like to think of it as a balance between looking up, looking in and looking out — just as you saw in the balance model in figure 1.

Looking up invites you to stop and smell the roses. Take stock of how you're working and what's happening in your life. Consider how a healthier version of yourself may better serve you.

There is a process constantly at play in our bodies called homeostasis.[2] The technical definition is 'a self-regulating process by which biological systems maintain stability while adjusting to changing external conditions.' Or, put another way, 'the ability or tendency to maintain internal stability in an organism to compensate for environmental changes.'

It is a biological response to our environment. Basically, our bodies are designed, hard-wired, to return us to a state of equilibrium and positive, healthy response when allowed to do so — keeping ourselves within certain pre-set limits ensures optimal health.

So, we need to look at the whole of us, not just the work version. That means taking care of sleep, diet and exercise regimes and general wellbeing. We must look up from the hamster wheel and remember to pay attention to our base health needs.

> *Your diet is not only what you eat.*

Blogger and podcaster Natalie Hodson writes, 'Your diet is not only what you eat. It's what you watch, what you listen to, what you read, and the people you hang around. Be mindful of the things you put into your body emotionally, spiritually, and physically'.[3] So, think about getting rid of the junk in your diet.

Let's tackle the foundational aspects of self-care.

Sleep is getting some good shut-eye

In my years as a clinical therapist, I worked with clients in the early stages of recovery from addiction. For years, they had passed out rather than fallen asleep. One of the very first elements for getting back on track is developing good sleep hygiene.

Essentially, that means forming a habit of self-care through careful attention to the process of going to bed and getting a good night's sleep. It's developing and maintaining a regular pattern of going to bed and getting up at the same time every day. And that includes weekends.

Even people who have not had a supportive, restful, quality sleep pattern (often for decades) find that the body and brain crave a systematic, habitual, predictable sleep pattern.

Within a very short period (I am talking days, not weeks), we can adapt to a new way of self-care through sleep. It is a remarkable display of physical resilience. The brain yearns for proper sleep, and grabs it when given the opportunity.

> *The brain yearns for proper sleep.*

The primary strategy to ensure a proper sleep hygiene practice is regularity. Choose a time to go to bed and stick to it. Choose when to get up and stick to it. Ensure a break from technology for about an hour before going to bed.

There's a wealth of evidence suggesting the benefits of journaling before going to bed. Journaling starts the sleep process as it enables you to leave your thoughts behind before you close your eyes.

Meditating is a somewhat new practice for me, but I am finding great value in it. I spend around ten to fifteen minutes meditating before going to sleep and the same upon waking. There's a wide range of meditation apps available to support this practice. One I often use has Tibetan singing bowls. It's a matter of focusing on the chime for as long as possible.

Many people worry that their brains are working too hard to meditate. They beat themselves up for being unable to rest or slow their minds. But if the idea of emptying your mind of all thought is stopping you from meditating, then don't worry. Jon Kabat-Zinn is an emeritus Professor of Medicine at the University of Massachusetts Medical School and a world leader in mindfulness. He says you cannot make your mind go blank. 'It would not be desirable because a blank mind — what is that? There's no awareness whatsoever.'[4]

A blank mind — what is that?

There are also some excellent 'body scan' and mindfulness and meditating apps that can help you focus on calming the mind and relaxing the body to allow you to sleep. My particular favourites are Insight Timer (for learning to meditate), Sleep Cycle (for sleeping, obviously), Headspace and Calm. Try them in whatever format you prefer and see what works for you.

These apps are superb if you wake in the middle of the night worrying, as many people do. Slipping into a body-scan meditation for ten to fifteen minutes can slow your mind and body so you can return to sleep.

The study of mindfulness has provided significant insights into the workings of the brain. Jon Kabat-Zinn is right; we can't expect our brains to stop doing what they are meant to do. The brain's job is to think and work constantly, but we can train ourselves to focus inward without judgement.

Acknowledge the distraction and return your focus.

Noticing your brain is racing means you are paying the right kind of attention. You acknowledge the distraction and return your focus. It really is that simple.

Other people recommend getting out of bed for a brief period if you are awake for longer than thirty minutes. The idea is that you return to bed as if you were going there for the first time that night.

Research indicates we need approximately seven to eight hours of sleep each night to be effective.[5] But I believe in quality over quantity, and six hours of sleep is far more helpful if you get to bed before midnight.

I find that bedtime after 9.30pm is a waste of time, as I am often just scrolling through social media or watching something on TV that I won't even remember. So, I go to bed and get up earlier to do something productive. It works for me!

Never underestimate the importance of good sleep. There is far more going on than just resting.

Never underestimate the importance of good sleep.

Research has discovered that the glymphatic system removes waste products from the brain and nervous system while we sleep. It uses cerebrospinal fluid to collect the waste (proteins, toxins etc.) and flushes them from the brain. It's a form of deep cleaning during deep sleep — taking out the trash. It doesn't happen at any other time, as the glymphatic system only kicks in when other bodily functions are at rest.[6] Science is also now discovering the role of an impaired glymphatic system in developing Alzheimer's Disease.[7]

Eating also affects sleep, especially if we overeat too close to bedtime or eat food that is too rich to be easily digested. That's because the energy is used to digest food rather than deep-clean the brain. Drinking alcohol also affects good sleep patterns.

Take a break from technology for about an hour before going to bed. Research shows that our circadian rhythms are all over the place when blue light from devices interferes with melatonin production.[8] And do you really need to read that snotty email from your boss just before you sleep? Some people advocate for wearing blue light glasses to counteract the harm. But recent research concluded that they did not improve objective measures of sleep time or sleep quality. It is far better to develop a good sleep hygiene practice than to try to find ways to thwart the system.[9]

Creating the right environment for sleep is simple.

> *If you want to change the world, start by making your bed.*

In his 2014 speech to the University of Texas, Admiral William McRaven said that if you want to change the world, start by making your bed.[10] Aside from the obvious reference to discipline and neatness, making your bed means you will have accomplished the first task of your day and set yourself up to achieve further successful outcomes.

To my mind, there is another element to this habit. Getting into a well-made bed is a joy and a pleasure, instead of wrestling messy sheets and doona to try to get comfortable. Even more profoundly, making your bed says you care about yourself and deserve this comfort.

Bedmaking can also be a surprising litmus test for other things that are not going so well. Noticing your bed isn't made can be a warning that other areas of your life are slipping as well. I hear it frequently when working with clients experiencing burnout and excessive stress. The first opportunity for self-care is missed and goes unnoticed until the end of the day. It takes less than a minute to make your bed. Try it and see the difference it makes.

Diet is not just what we eat

'The road to health is paved with good intestines'

— Sherry A. Rogers

This is not a dietary advice book, so I'm not going to extol any alleged virtues of calorie control, and I'm not going to tell you to eat your vegetables. There is a wealth of information available about what is good to eat. Some people follow vegetarian and vegan diets, while others espouse gluten-free, paleo and other restrictive diets. I'm not here to talk about any of those.

In his book *Homo Deus*, Yuval Noah Harari explains that humans are the only species on Earth that cannot or do not feed themselves properly. Three times more of us will die from too much food than not enough.[11] That is a huge revelation, given we have so much information about what we can and should be doing to support ourselves through what we eat.

So, there is a hugely valuable and essential element to a good diet that we need to consider.

Tell me. Do you ever forget to eat a meal? Do you ever forget to drink water? Do you need to snack on sugary snacks at three o'clock in the afternoon?

The pointed responses to these questions in my workshops tell me these issues are widespread.

Consider your answer. Do you need to take better care of your diet?

Just like good sleep patterns, we must also establish good eating patterns.

The gastrointestinal tract (GIT) is where everything (except air) that feeds and sustains enters the body. Every vitamin, mineral and amino acid (except the eight created internally) enters through this system. And we treat it abominably! Not only do we not provide what the body needs to function effectively, but we ingest stuff that abuses it.

Have you ever gone to take out the little food recycling bag on your benchtop, only to find it is rancid and gooey? Imagine what is happening in your gut.

Later in this chapter, we will explore the gut and brain connection in greater detail when we discuss the enteric nervous system.

Water

Are you drinking enough water? I'm sure you know about the necessity for proper hydration. Still, there are benefits beyond the obvious, particularly when it comes to regulating and reducing chronic stress levels and burnout.

Water helps to regulate stress hormones, like cortisol, which trigger the stress response. Dehydration increases cortisol, making it harder to deal with everyday challenges and issues.

Water also flushes out neurotoxins. That process regulates the stress response and improves blood circulation, thereby supporting oxygen distribution to where it is needed.

Water transports minerals, vitamins and oxygen to the brain. It also helps to support and maintain the process of neurogenesis (essentially, rebuilding our brains with new neurons and removing old nervous system cells).

> *Water is your friend.*

If weight loss or weight control is part of your self-care plan, you need to know that water is your friend. Water is a natural appetite suppressant, helping you eat less, snack less and digest properly. Water also speeds up your metabolism, increasing the rate at which you burn calories.

Emeran Mayer, the author of the *Mind-Gut Connection*, says the gut has capabilities that surpass all other organs and even rival the brain.[12] The gut has its own nervous system (the enteric nervous system, or ENS). It is often referred to as the second brain and has as many nerve cells as the spinal column. But the most compelling feature of the ENS is that it produces a substantial proportion of the neurotransmitters and brain chemicals required to combat stress and maintain good brain health.

In short, a massive population of microbes and bacteria resides in the gut. Estimates suggest there are ten times more microbial cells in the human gut than in the whole human body, totalling roughly

100 trillion microbes, representing as many as 5,000 different species and weighing approximately two kilograms.[13] If that's not enough to put you off your grub, then keep reading.

Recent research by Johns Hopkins Medicine found that a 'higher than usual percentage of people with irritable bowel syndrome and functional bowel problems will develop depression and anxiety, at levels much higher than in the general population'.[14] [15]

This is worth remembering as you read the next sections, where we'll consider the four main hormones, dopamine, serotonin, endorphins and oxytocin. I call them the *happy hormones* because they relate to mood stabilisation, reward, satisfaction and connection with others.

Dopamine

Dopamine is the feel-good neurotransmitter. It travels through the bloodstream and drives our reward system. Basically, it rewards us for doing stuff that supports our survival or anything that feels pleasant. That is why a cold drink on a hot day feels so good. A nice meal we want to eat again. A fire on a cold night, shelter from the weather. Sex. A good night's sleep. Listening to soothing music. Essentially, any action that tells us it's good for survival.

> *Dopamine is like a pat on the back.*

Dopamine is like a pat on the back for a job well done.

Of course, nothing in life is that simple. The downside is when alcohol or other drugs are used to cope with the shit in our lives. Our brains quickly connect the dots and love to remind us that these work to alleviate suffering but can quickly hijack the system in seeking the pleasure reward. (The psychologists reading this will see operant conditioning forming.)

Remember, your dopamine levels are created in the brain and the gut, so you are what you eat. Any pleasant self-care activity that grabs you will increase your dopamine response — just try to pick the healthy ones. Acknowledge and celebrate the little wins. These are great for managing stress levels.

Serotonin

Serotonin is a mood stabiliser that improves sleep and reduces and controls anxiety and happiness. It is a neurotransmitter produced in nerve cells to carry signals between nerve cells and is found mainly in the digestive system. Again, we are what we eat.

You may have heard of the widely used depression treatment called SSRI – Selective Serotonin Reuptake Inhibitor. Without going too far down this rabbit hole, SSRIs support brain chemistry by slowing down the body's reabsorption of serotonin in the system, making it more readily available when needed.

This treatment supports anxiety and depression, and the same prescription is often used for both conditions. 'Depression and anxiety are flip sides of the same coin', says Nancy B. Irwin, 'as being depressed can make us anxious, and anxiety often causes depression.'[16] Makes sense.

To increase your serotonin levels, get out in the sun, do some cardio exercise, maybe get a massage, and eat properly.

Serotonin is like a warm, fuzzy feeling.

Endorphins

We'll talk more about endorphins and their role in stress levels in the exercise section, but for now, know that endorphins are the brain's natural painkiller and steroid and are close cousins of dopamine. The brain releases endorphins to reduce pain and stress and increase pleasure, while dopamine is slowly released to boost your mood afterwards.

To increase your endorphins, get some exercise, have a good laugh, meditate, eat some indulgent dark chocolate or have a glass of red wine (or both!).

Endorphins are like a 'giddy-up' to alleviate discomfort and allow good feelings.

Oxytocin

Oxytocin is the bonding hormone. We'll discuss it in depth in a later chapter, given the value and survival necessity of forming close relationships with others. Oxytocin is released when we feel connected to people. A powerful example is skin-to-skin contact between a mother and her newborn infant.

To increase or stimulate oxytocin, spend time with friends, pet your dog or cat, play with a baby, and invest time in other people. Have sex or cook a meal for a loved one who will appreciate it. (Or both!) Hug your family, or pay someone a compliment.

Oxytocin is like a warm hug or a good cuddle.

The brain relies on two main mood-related hormones for mood stabilising and resisting chronic stress (dopamine and serotonin). Fifty per cent of your dopamine and ninety-five per cent of your serotonin are created in the gut. What supports their production, of course, is a healthy diet.

We know our gut biome craves sugar when we create a diet heavily loaded with sugar. So sugar cravings are partly around healthy digestion but also the gut biome crying out for what it is used to getting.[17]

Your body needs you to eat regularly. Three times a day is likely ideal and manageable for most people. There are plenty of theories and programs related to this idea. You may prefer to follow an intermittent fasting program, but some don't like to eat in the morning — and you really should. Or you may follow a different regime. Whatever works for you, as long as it serves you and isn't restricting your self-care or harming your health. And make sure you are not using it to beat yourself up.

We all know what healthy food looks like.

We need to ensure that we are eating properly. We all know what healthy food looks like. In simplest terms, if it *comes from a plant*, that is good. If it is *manufactured in a plant*, perhaps not so much. The gut needs the best opportunity to create as much dopamine and serotonin as possible to support the brain to combat excessive stress levels.

Stress can increase inflammation in the body by affecting the gut microbes. The vagus nerve is constantly being hacked by gut bacteria, which interferes with how much dopamine and serotonin can get to our brains in the bidirectional gut-brain axis.

The usual good foods support the system, so prebiotics, probiotics, etc., create the right environment to generate the levels of dopamine and serotonin that our brains will need.

When we are not eating, forget to eat, eat crap food, or are under increasing levels of stress or burnout, energy tends to come from our adrenal system. Basically, the fight or flight response provides the energy required to keep moving. But that's not good because it uses different energy sources, namely adrenaline and cortisol.

We know that overuse of those hormones in response to the environment creates all kinds of health issues, such as inflammation in the body, gut and digestion problems, cardiovascular issues and other adverse health conditions. If we create stress hormones through our perceived response to stress or danger and don't use them up, they hang around in our systems, causing havoc.

The other point about relying on the adrenal system for energy is that it pulls blood flow from the digestive system and sends it to the body's extremities — as if we were in danger. The digestive system won't work because it's turned off when our adrenal nervous system (ANS) is switched on.

This ANS (fight or flight) response doesn't know the difference between danger and stress, so it's just responding as it always has. It's an efficient system that keeps us safe. It takes absolutely no chances and hasn't evolved to the same extent as our environment.

If we're constantly resisting or fighting danger, we're using the wrong energy source and causing untold levels of harm to our bodies.

Adrenal overload and fatigue

The jury is still out as to whether adrenal fatigue exists. Whichever side of the fence you are on, whether you view it as a thyroid issue or adrenal overload, wiser people have been locked in this debate for some time. But we can measure the cortisol levels in our systems at given times, and something is happening to throw it out of kilter.

Long story short, we must develop a good habit of eating regularly and well. Not just for energy and dietary support but to ensure we are armed with the best defence against stress.

Exercise

I've said this is not a dietary advice book, and nor is it an exercise manual. There is a wealth of information available on what constitutes a supportive and valuable exercise regime, so I don't intend to saw the sawdust on what we should be doing to meet our exercise needs.

However, I would say that there are robust correlations between mood-stabilising hormones, brain health and the role of exercise in good brain health. The brain is not just a computer; it is a living, breathing organ that requires exercise and good health like any other organ in the body. We can harm the brain as easily as we support it.

Endorphins are often referred to as the 'exerciser's high' — that feeling of elation that comes when exercising and pushing ourselves to our limits.

But endorphins do so much more.[18]

They play a significant role in supporting how our bodies relate to stress (for example, in controlling the pituitary gland and inhibiting or releasing adrenaline). Endorphins also act as a natural pain reliever and sedative.[19] They strengthen the brain by supporting memory and cognitive function, promoting neurogenesis (replacing brain cells and regeneration of the brain) and neuroplasticity (the brain's ability to adapt to needs).

> *Exercise plays a considerable role in self-care.*

Exercise plays a considerable role in self-care for reasons beyond increasing fitness levels. Endorphins have many benefits for the body, including reduced pain and discomfort, better mood and self-esteem, and increased pleasure.

Let's look at ways to sneak some exercise into your day that you may not have considered.

The fake commute. This fabulous concept was born during the Covid lockdowns, around early 2021. We've realised that the traditional commute to work has few positive aspects and no real upside (unless you walked or cycled to work and it formed part of your exercise regime). The commute was generally a very stressful time that book-ended an already stressful day.

Perhaps you, like many others, now start work during the time that you would typically commute. While there's nothing wrong with doing so, it tends to blur the lines between work and home life. And, if you already don't switch off easily, then you need to develop a practice that can easily separate and define the two roles.

In the Introduction, I highlighted the compounding effects of working during this commute time. You can end up working an extra month per year! Again, there is nothing wrong with doing so, as long as you temper it with self-care and work-life balance.

Essentially, the fake commute consists of getting ready for your working day as usual. But, before you sit at your desk or table (and after you have made your bed!), head out the door and walk briskly for fifteen to twenty minutes.

I started this habit in lockdown and can attest that it is a marvellous start to the day. A lot happens when your system is warmed up and fired up properly. I spend the time thinking about my day, planning what I need to do and perhaps pondering a problem. Others use it to listen to a podcast or as a form of movement meditation.

In those twenty minutes, I cover two kilometres, sort out much of what is on my mind, and arrive home with a plan for how my day will go. If I am not going to the gym, for a beach walk or a swim later, I repeat the fake commute at the end of my day.

If you develop this practice, you will find that, in a short space of time:

- Your fitness level improves because you have walked up to twenty kilometres more than you would otherwise have walked in the week.
- You have lost no personal time (you would have been commuting at this time anyway).
- You have planned your day or caught up on a podcast and saved time there too.
- You have used the time to walk the dog or spent valuable time with your partner.
- You have focused on your self-care.

- You have segregated work time from your time and developed a solid work-home separation and work-life balance.
- You have woken up properly, with fresh air and exercise to commence your day in the right frame of mind.

Another practice I have embarked on is the daily **two-minute plank.** It started as a thirty-day challenge, but I have extended it as part of my beginning and end of day rituals, which include a few minutes of stretching. I am astonished at the difference it has made. Just a 60-90 second plank before my fake commute walk and again before going to bed. Try it. (If you feel like it, add in five or ten push-ups.)

Heart rate variability

Another measure worth mentioning here is heart rate variability (HRV).

HRV is measured by the variation in the beat-to-beat intervals between heartbeats. So, rather than counting individual heartbeats, the focus is on the minute time or space between heartbeats as a measure of fitness or stress response. These fluctuations can indicate current or future health problems, including heart conditions and mental health issues like anxiety and depression.

HRV is measured by the variation in the beat-to-beat intervals between heartbeats.

Studies into HRV and training to improve stress and performance responses have shown significantly lower cortisol and skin conductance levels (the electrical conductivity of the skin that allows us to measure the levels of the autonomic nervous system activity) in experimental groups compared with control groups.[20]

Many smartwatches offer HRV measurement, so you might consider it another measure of your progress directly related to your stress levels.

Over to you

In summary, you can do much to support your physical health. It is all related to mental and brain health and dramatically affects your mindset.

To travel safely and competently, we want a smooth-running engine.

To travel safely and competently, we want a smooth-running engine.

So, take time to look up from your hamster wheel, conveyor belt, or rat race, and ask what you can do with the information in this chapter to better support yourself.

Grab your action plan (see the link to my website at the back of the book), commit, be accountable to someone and start your new practice. We will keep adding to this as we go.

CHAPTER TWO

Burnout Makes Me Wish I Had More Middle Fingers

'Burnout is about your workplace, not your people.'

— Jennifer Moss

Questions: Do you feel exhausted? The kind of exhaustion that doesn't go away after a good night's sleep? Are you emotionally tired as well? Do you have brain fog or feel you are losing your sharpness? Are you cynical or apathetic, or have a good old-fashioned case of the 'fuck-its'?

Burnout is very much at the forefront of people's minds today. It appears to have become the primary mental health challenge for individuals, teams and organisations.

In this chapter, we will examine what burnout is and what it isn't and how it might present itself.

I am constantly asked about the steps to overcome and recover from burnout, and the answers lie in everything you are reading here.

In a 2019 Harvard Business Review article, Jennifer Moss described work-related burnout as about your workplace, not your people. It is not a personal issue. It's an organisational issue.[1] Moss means we need to look at work design, workload, work suitability, autonomy and clarity of roles. Her point is that we can't blame the person.

I often refer to burnout as the canary in the cage. That may be a tired metaphor but stay with me as I have a slight twist to it. Historically, coal mines used a canary to detect a toxic work environment with (for example) overwhelming carbon monoxide gas. When the canary collapsed, it was a signal to abandon the mine and escape until it was safe to return.

Today, we can't blame the canary for collapsing the mine. And we cannot keep looking for stronger canaries. Sometimes we have to look at the coal mine and what's happening in the toxic workplace. More on this shortly.

We cannot keep looking for stronger canaries.

Many philosophical arguments question whether an organisation is a product or the accumulated result of the people working there. So, in some sense, burnout might be a people issue. But Jennifer Moss is saying it's a system problem, and sometimes we must look at the dance rather than the dancers.

My own experience

I experienced burnout for the first time many years ago, and it has happened more than once since then. The thing with burnout is that if you experience it once, you are more susceptible to succumbing to it again. However, every cloud has a silver lining, and the next time you should be able to spot it coming much sooner. Small comfort, but there you go.

In Chapter Eleven, we'll discuss boundaries, as that is where I fell short. I didn't have clear boundaries around my mental health and capabilities and just wanted to deliver the best results possible. Whatever the cost.

While I didn't see it coming the first time, I certainly did the second and could better deal with it. My very understanding business partner (and dear friend), Peter, supported me through it. It took a mindset shift, a focus on my resilience, and a deep dive into self-care to make the difference the second time.

I discovered that one of my triggers was my mobile phone ringtone. I grew to detest and almost fear it. That was back when you didn't have much choice around ringtone possibilities. Peter's solution was to tell me to throw my phone in the rubbish bin. I could get a new one when I was ready. It was an extraordinarily generous offer but completely impractical. However, it did speak to his level of care for me, and I've never forgotten it. I think I've learned more about life from Peter than anyone else.

Interestingly, I still change my ringtone every couple of months. Just in case it becomes a trigger.

When we don't focus enough on living a balanced life, elements can overtake or overthrow our awareness, and we may not even notice them creeping up on us.

When working from home (even occasionally), we know that blending work and home means we don't switch off. Or we continue working longer than we would have done if we were going to a workplace.

Or we certainly think about work in that combined environment of work and home. It can become quite a habit to walk past your laptop and give the mouse or touchpad a quick flick to see what emails have come in since you logged off.

In late 2021, I met someone who took the unusual (but effective) step of throwing a towel over her laptop at the end of her day, just as we used to cover the budgie cage at night so the bird would stop singing. (I'm not sure what she threw over her smartphone.) Looking at her laptop again required removing the towel and switching the computer out of sleep mode. Those two actions meant she had to stop and think about what she was doing and could change her mind.

These could well be the points where we appreciate that we are not exercising self-care and could be heading towards burnout — if we even see it happening. The first interesting point is that, quite often, someone else may see the symptoms and signs in us before we spot them ourselves.

Let's explore this in some detail.

The canary in the coal mine

Applying the analogy of the canary in the coal mine to your situation may be helpful.

Think about your coal mine — your workplace, work or role, whichever helps. What would you say is your toxic environment?

Now, think about your toxic gas. Down the coal mine, it was carbon monoxide, a gas you couldn't see, hear, smell, taste or touch. It didn't trigger any of the five senses, so the miners didn't know it was there until they were overcome by it.

You probably won't have a toxic gas to worry about, but there could well be an invisible source of harm that makes it a dangerous place to be. Is it your workload, constant or increasing stress, or a lack of autonomy in how you do your job? Perhaps it's a lack of clarity about what is expected of you. Poor leadership, maybe? Maybe an unfair workload compared to others in the team, or you feel discriminated against, bullied, or stigmatised for some reason. It might be a lack of team collaboration, cohesion, or tense relationships between a few team members.

A lot can go wrong, and we often make the best of a bad situation, but this creates a difficult work environment.

When they noticed the canary had stopped singing (they used male canaries because they would sing incessantly to seek a mate, even down a dark mine), the coalminers responded immediately for their safety.

Think about what your canary might be. What gives you a signal that all is not well? Is it your stress levels, irritability and tiredness? Do you begin isolating yourself and avoiding certain people? Perhaps you drink a little more than usual or engage in other coping strategies that may not serve you well in the long term.

> *What gives you a signal that all is not well?*

Or maybe your canary is a person? Someone you work with. Maybe it is your leader. When they begin to react to their stress levels, is it a signal that all is not well for the rest of you?

It is highly likely that you ignore your canary and keep pushing on. That seems crazy, but I see it all the time. And it involves your self-critic, saying you should be able to deal with this level of adversity. Everyone else seems to be able to, so why can't you? (The self-critic is a more extensive subject we will explore in a later chapter.)

Or you tell yourself you are just tired, and if you can just make it to the weekend and get some rest, you'll be fine. Or maybe after the end-of-month results come in. Or the end-of-quarter is fast approaching. Perhaps at the end of the financial year, when all the targets go back to zero, you can catch up then. There's a big break coming up at Christmas, so that will have to do....

Stop and consider whether you (or someone close to you) are more than tired or exhausted. Is there more to the feeling than just a lack of energy? If so, that may be your first clue.

The official definition

According to World Health Organization (WHO) and the definition in the International Classification of Databases, edition 11 (ICD-11), three main domains or syndrome symptoms need to be recognised to meet the official definition of burnout. And we need to meet all three criteria.

Burnout is defined in ICD-11 as follows.

> 'Burnout is a syndrome conceptualized as resulting from chronic workplace stress that has not been successfully managed. It is characterized by three dimensions:

- feelings of energy depletion or exhaustion
- increased mental distance from one's job, or feelings of negativism or cynicism related to one's job, and
- reduced professional efficacy.' [2]

The first domain, exhaustion, is largely self-explanatory, but it can be broken into three different segments — mental, physical and emotional. All and any of these can present in a burnout situation.

The second vital element is cynicism. That means a level of disengagement or mental distance, sometimes seen as resentment that builds up against the organisation, the leaders, the team, or the clients. If clients and customers are involved, this can be dangerous and present a risk to the reputation of the organisation, the team, the individual and the leader.

According to WHO, the third dimension speaks to efficacy, which is the ability to be effective and deliver the expected quality of work.

What is missing from this equation is the effects on individual mental health. We will explore this later in the chapter.

Cynicism can spread like Covid

When cynicism rises, individuals begin to speak negatively or disparagingly about the organisation, the team, the workload, the leaders, or the clients. And when this happens, burnout can become contagious because negative talk can spread quickly through the team — particularly if it's a relentless conversation.

The issue with cynicism is that the person experiencing it finds themselves (consciously or not) in an unhealthy and lonely space. They don't want to be alone in that space, prompting cynical conversations and behaviour. Or they will seek to validate these feelings by attempting to enlist others into similar behaviours.

I view this more as apathy than cynicism, because if people remain passionate about their role, their burnout experience may have origins outside of the workplace. It displays a lack of interest and diminished enthusiasm we would expect of a passionate person beyond scepticism, cynicism or resentment.

It often also happens that their efficacy or ability to deliver good work can be affected. They may be disappointed in themselves, as they can no longer deliver work they want to be proud of. They find themselves needing to read emails several times, missing salient points in an argument, and forgetting or confusing deadlines or names. Brain fog starts to occur, undermining the quality and ability to deliver their best work.

A new model of burnout

Gordon Parker, Scientia Professor of Psychiatry at the University of New South Wales, and his colleagues, Gabriela Tavella and Kerrie Eyers, recently released an excellent book called *Burnout. A Guide to Identifying Burnout and Pathways to Recovery.*[3]

They argue that the WHO definition of burnout doesn't meet today's reckonings. Their new definition has as many as twelve criteria.

I agree, so I've added a fourth element to the burnout definition that incorporates some of their findings and includes what I feel was missing.

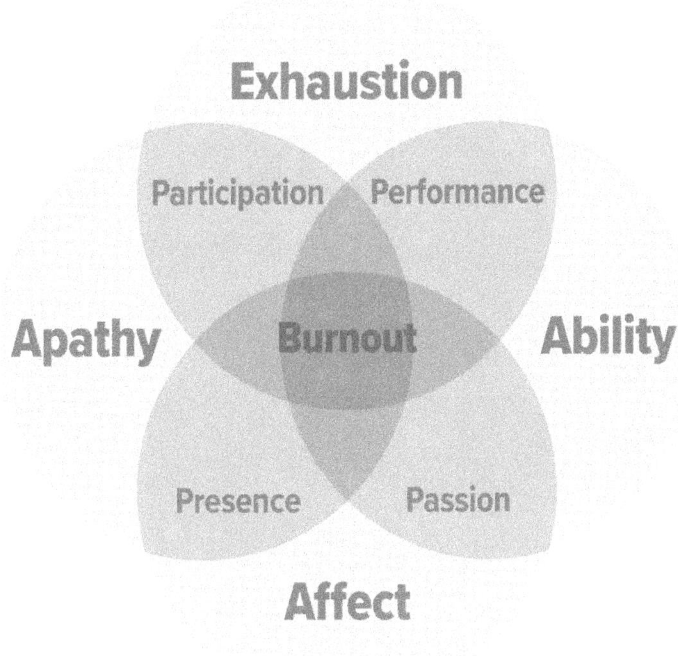

Figure 2: Aspects of burnout

Parker and his colleagues determined that the ICD-11 official definition contained nothing substantial related to mental health. Nor was it in the description offered by Maslach, Leiter, and Jackson in the early 1980s. (They were the creators of the Maslach Burnout Inventory, or MBI, the definitive burnout measurement tool.)

The prevailing wisdom did not seem to speak directly to the mindset or mental health of people who may be dealing with, struggling with, or being challenged by some level of burnout.

I have attempted to encompass this notion of mental health and depression and anxiety in people experiencing burnout by using the term 'affect'. In psychological terms, 'affect' is like a particular kind of influence, or something's ability to influence our mind with the result that we develop an emotional response. Both mood and emotion are considered 'affective states'.

It's like an overt expression of internal emotions and a visible reaction to physical circumstances. And there is no doubt that when we experience these as a result of experiencing burnout, that can have a long-lasting effect.

Research from Lamers et al., shows that more than sixty per cent of people who do not address these mental health challenges promptly can go on to develop a secondary mental health issue.[4] That's what we would call a comorbid or co-occurring condition.

Burnout at work

The intersections in my burnout model (figure 2) all refer to something lacking. In other words, lack of performance is at the intersection of exhaustion and your ability to deliver good work.

A lack of passion develops between the ability to deliver good work and affect (or the outward expression of internal emotions). It looks like apathy or a case of the 'fuck-its'.

When apathy and affect coincide, we see a lack of presence or an absence of presenting your best self. (The WHO definition of burnout talks of cynicism, but I think apathy is closer as it is both internal and externally focused.)

Work-related burnout can result from someone having little control over their work. In other words, a lack of autonomy or a lack of a decision-making element to their role. Perhaps a sense that they don't have much impact or control over what they do.

Where we're not putting our best foot forward, despite our best efforts, the outcome of an intersection or an interaction between exhaustion and apathy is a lack of participation.

When we experience a lack of recognition or don't feel we're rewarded sufficiently for our work, we feel like hamsters on a wheel.

> *We feel like hamsters on a wheel.*

Correspondingly, burnout can occur if work is chaotic or we are in a high-pressure workplace with constant and ongoing stress levels. Historically, burnout was measured in the health sector and seen as a work-related issue. It spoke to how people in the health sector developed what's known as vicarious or secondary trauma and compassion fatigue (an even more destructive case of the 'fuck-its').

But we now know that other factors can involve a level of burnout. Parker and his colleagues also highlighted this point, saying that lifestyle or personality can influence whether or not we experience burnout.[5]

Quiet quitting

While quiet quitting is a relatively new term, the idea has long been known in union circles as 'work to rule' and is used as a form of industrial action.

The recent social media buzz of 'quiet quitting' relates to the idea that we no longer will tolerate going above and beyond for a leader or company that doesn't recognise us, or we have to keep advertising our value. People take back their time and self-care by only doing what they are contracted to do. It is a silent protest at being overworked and leaders who expect more and more from their teams without reasonable reward.

We work to live rather than live to work.

Having started to review our lives and decided that we work to live rather than live to work, we are limiting work to what is written in our job descriptions. That means we take back time to spend on ourselves and those closest to us. This is Self-Care 101 and the premise behind my next book (stay tuned!).

Whether you're taking this step because you're burning out or through a sense of fairness, then big hugs, high-fives and best wishes to you from me! I am on your team and in your corner.

But, let's unpack the concept of quiet quitting a little further because I can see a few potholes ahead.

I love that people are doing this to improve their self-care and self-compassion because that is how we set healthy boundaries and decide what is good for us and what isn't.

But the first pothole with quiet quitting is that we keep our boundaries secret. Why be quiet about it? A boundary that nobody knows about may as well not be there. The only person who will have an issue with your boundary is someone who stands to gain by you not having it!

The second pothole is that you need to be satisfied with where your career is at. If you decide to do the minimum required, you may be overlooked for promotion. You won't be noticed for the 'right' reasons and could be the first to go in a round of redundancies. It's far better to talk with your leader about being fairly compensated for your work —

particularly if you have been working above and beyond for some time. You have already proven yourself worthy. You know what to do if you get the usual response of promotion freezes and funding constraints. Your self-care, mental health and wellbeing cannot become victims of an organisation's inability to fund a sufficient workforce.

If the word quitting is in your vocabulary, then you may already have one foot out the door. That third pothole can be hard to come back from. So, are you quitting, or are you taking a stand?

Leaders, if you are seeing this in any of your people, it is far better to explore than be punitive about it. Remember that Jennifer Moss described work-related burnout as an organisational issue, not personal. It will be related to work design, workload, clarity, uncertain or unfair expectations or a shortfall in tools to do the job.

If your head is in quiet quitting, don't be quiet about it and don't quit until you've had a conversation. If the conversation doesn't go as you need it to, then your wellbeing, mental health and self-care need to come first. And nobody should be surprised.

Burnout outside work

When we talk about lifestyle, I mean a lack of balance between work and the rest of your life. It might be a lack of close relationships or taking on too much. Working too long or too hard and poor sleep hygiene can all have a debilitating effect on energy levels and the four precursors to burnout. Think about those who, during Covid lockdowns, found home-schooling particularly challenging. Caring for family members with special needs, such as children or elderly parents, can all have a bearing and lead to burnout.

Perfectionism seems to be an outstanding problem that can lead to burnout. That's where people feel they must strive hard to deliver good results and when good enough is not good enough. It can be the result of residual anxiety levels that they struggle with on a day-to-day basis.

Burnout in and of itself is an occupational phenomenon, not a health condition. In other words, you cannot go to your GP and get a diagnosis of burnout because it isn't a clinical or medical condition. Your GP may diagnose health issues arising from burnout, such as cardiovascular problems, digestive issues, or poor sleep hygiene due to excessive stress, but not burnout itself.

Stress is often confused with burnout, but stress is just a state of being, and we need a certain amount of it to function effectively. We will examine resilience in a later chapter, but for now, imagine stress as a violin string. If it isn't under enough tension, it is useless and doesn't work. Too much, and it will snap. With manageable stress levels, the violin string produces a beautiful result.

Recovery

The obvious question arises. How do I recover from burnout?

Figure 3: Recovery from burnout

I see three stages for somebody to come back from the experience of burnout.

Parker, Tavella and Eyers offered the excellent analogy of a flickering candle. How we respond to a flickering candle and how we reignite a candle that is already extinguished, are very different processes.

As with any early intervention or prevention strategy, the earlier we deal with burnout, the better the outcome.

And it should begin with self-care.

It starts with restoring good physical and mental health, a positive mindset and developing resilience. That ignites the ability to review workload, work design, work balance, the clarity of roles, suitability for a role, and other KPIs by which the role may be measured.

Jennifer Moss refers to this when she says it's not enough to leave work to the individual. We're better when we have clarity around what's expected of us. That inspires us to become more engaged and motivated and return to what we once were. Resilience improves, and we find ourselves recovering. It doesn't always mean changing jobs, but don't rule that out.

To achieve clarity, we must understand that team members need to trust each other. And we need to know, as individuals, that we are respected, belong, and feel safe in the company of others when we're not at our best. All of these are manifestly important to somebody recovering from burnout.

For a team to be optimal, or embrace somebody who is struggling, we need to know it is okay to not be okay for a while.

Bessel van der Kolk is a global leader in trauma recovery. He writes that being able to feel safe with other people is the single most critical aspect of mental health.[6] I believe he is right.

We often see burnout in somebody else before we see it in ourselves. That's because our self-critic makes excuses and chastises us for feeling burnt out rather than having self-compassion to understand that we are under considerable duress and need support. Just like the cliché of the plumber's tap that leaks, we are far better at seeing another person's struggles than admitting to our own.

Consider the following questions and apply them to your self-care action plan. Commit to exploring some of the elements of burnout to see if they fit you, then be accountable to somebody else in your field so you can understand that burnout is real.

Burnout is everybody's business. It is far more prevalent than we are prepared to admit.

Thankfully, the return from burnout can be swift if it is dealt with quickly and correctly.

Don't lose hope.

Burnout is everybody's business.

Questions to ask yourself

Do you lose track of your train of thought?

Do you no longer have time to engage in your favourite hobbies?

Are you fully present and engaged in conversations with your partner or others?

Are you getting enough sleep?

Do you feel exhausted, even if you've had a good night's sleep?

Do you forget to eat, or eat rubbish because you don't have time?

Do you often feel a knot in your stomach?

Do you ever feel a tightness in your chest?

Are you dropping the ball on commitments?

Are you detached from life outside work?

Do you find yourself being short or rude to people?

CHAPTER THREE

If Anxiety Burned Calories, I'd Be Unstoppable

'People aren't born strong. People grow strong little by little, encountering difficult situations and learning not to run from them.'

— Christina Grimmie

Questions: What are the most common causes of my anxiety? Do I worry about the past or the future? Or both? Am I worried about what people will think of me? What are my signals? (Full disclosure, my fingernails do the measuring for me. They are the barometer for my anxiety levels. I can't really call them battle scars, but, in many ways, they are.)

The interesting thing about anxiety is that it could sit in any of the three sections of this book. In terms of Looking Up, self-care and developing habits that keep the engine running, we can do many things to prevent or reduce our anxious state. Sleep, exercise and eating well play significant roles and impact the levels of brain chemicals related to mood and good function.

When we Look In, meditation, mindfulness practices, getting sufficient rest, and ensuring we engage in enjoyable activities that bring a bit of light relief can all reduce the incidence of anxiety.

Even in the third section, where we Look Out, we can adopt strategies in our relationships with others that support us when we experience anxiety. In Part Three, we'll delve into boundaries, which are hugely important for self-support, and explore emotional intelligence, self-compassion and empathy.

No one has greater empathy for an anxious person than someone who experiences it.

In this chapter, I'll talk about anxiety mostly from a sub-clinical perspective (i.e., not diagnosed but undoubtedly present), as this is where many of us live. In particular, I will be pushing the idea of 'avoiding avoidance' as a strategy, as avoiding exacerbates and fuels anxiety.

Anxiety has its place

Dr Tracy Dennis-Tiwary is an anxiety researcher and professor of psychology and neuroscience. In her book *Future Tense: Why Anxiety is Good For You (Even Though It Feels Bad)*, she writes that anxiety can be misunderstood and needs a mindset shift. It isn't always debilitating, and the more we avoid and suppress it, the more it can spiral out of control.[1]

Dr Dennis-Tiwary correctly says that anxiety is an emotion we have evolved to experience. This ability to think into the future, plan, consider alternatives, seek opportunities in adversity, dream, and have a vision is hugely valuable.

Anxiety can help us be more innovative and creative and give us an edge over others if we learn to tame it. It does not need to be a hindrance or a malfunction. When we look at it as part of being human and an opportunity to corral our reserves to strive for greatness, it can take on a whole new meaning.

Anxiety is becoming far more prevalent in society and is here to stay, so let's make anxiety our ally rather than a feared enemy. But we have a dim view of anxiety, and we must explore that before adopting this newer approach.

Let's make anxiety our ally.

Whether you are generally anxious or only go to that place occasionally, you'll recognise that familiar feeling of dread and gnawing stomach that often comes without a specific reason.

Growing anxiety

A report by the Mental Health Commission of New South Wales in early 2022 suggests that one in eight Australians is experiencing a brand-new mental health challenge due to the uncertainty around Covid-19 — something they have never experienced before.[2]

I was recently engaged in advanced suicide prevention training with a group of general practitioner doctors. In conversation, I asked how much of their work was related to mental health. There were two parts to their answer — they reckoned about ten to fifteen per cent of their patients, but mental health comprised around seventy-five per cent of their work.

The doctors said people come for treatment complaining of digestion issues, problems with sleeping, and anger outbursts. Often, the patients cannot specify a mental health challenge until the doctor explores the possibility. People feel a stigma and a sensitivity to being seen as 'less-than', even when talking with their GP.

Treating mental health issues can take up to five times longer than dealing with a physical ailment. We see similar statistics in the workplace around sick leave taken for recovery from mental health issues.

The same but different

The symptoms of depression and anxiety are often so similar that the medical treatment can be the same. That was certainly my experience.

At the age of ten, I developed anxiety that was incorrectly diagnosed as depression. Without going too far down this rabbit hole (I could fill another book with this story!) I had an acute illness that made me very sick for a few months. Having just watched a TV episode of Little House on The Prairie, where the sister needed an operation and nearly died, I went into the hospital, convinced that was my destiny too. Frankly, I was shitting myself. It didn't help that I was the only kid in an adult male ward, but it did mean I got my own ashtray on my bedside locker. (I'm not kidding!)

The hospital staff were wonderful (aren't they all?), but, as then was the way in Ireland, all hospitals were faith-based and run by religious orders. I admit I didn't leave with as much admiration for the nuns running the wards as I did the doctors and nurses. A feverish, dangerously ill, ten-year-old boy, in fear of his life, was ripe for picking, and the nuns rolled out the fire and brimstone dogma with great enthusiasm. Needless to say, I didn't join in with the same level of eagerness; mine was more fear-based, but that didn't seem to matter. All roads led to Rome.

The only treatment I received for my fear and terror was the encouragement to 'Say my prayers'. Oh, and Holy Communion. I was 'asked' every morning if I wanted Holy Communion, but before I could answer, my bed sheets were tucked in (so I couldn't move) by two nurses racing about eight feet ahead of the priest, who swiftly completed the process. The whole thing was over in about two minutes, and I was 'safe' for another day, as long as I kept saying my prayers. Specifically, in my mind, it needed more prayers than I'd said the day before in case I was seen as slacking off!

And the end result? A young boy with crippling obsessive compulsive disorder and specific phobia anxiety — all of which were diagnosed as depression. Apparently, ten-year-old boys didn't get anxiety then — that was considered the domain of housewives.

I was thus set up with a predilection for anxiety and self-soothing behaviours that were not the healthiest for a young lad, although I did eventually get my smoking and drinking under control. I often wondered what happened to that nun. She'll have passed on to her afterlife by now, very possibly reading this and smiling *up* at me.

Making meaning of our world

We need to make meaning of what we see, feel and experience. It's an evolutionary throwback; we are a meaning-making species and need to understand our experience. When we didn't, we appointed gods to explain the unknown and the gaps in our logic.

We come to conclusions based on what we observe and recognise, and we do so from a very young age.

This useful background introduces one concept of how people learn to become anxious. I have seen it play out in countless therapy programs and client sessions over the years, particularly in people with addiction issues who develop unhealthy coping behaviours to soothe unexplained feelings and emotions.

Let's take a typical scenario — a very young child seeking approval from parents and carers. (We thrive on accolades and acceptance, to know our place in the tribe and to know we belong and are safe.) After painting a crayon or watercolour picture (usually pretty shit, but it was their best effort), the child presents it to the parent. But it doesn't get the desired approval, as the parent is distracted. It doesn't end up on the fridge door with the sibling's picture.

One-off incidents don't seem to matter adversely if the child experiences and receives consistent approval and acceptance. But if this 'perceived rejection' occurs regularly, the child makes meaning of the feeling of rejection. They assume they aren't good enough. The only solution is to work harder at being accepted, as they now feel unsafe and could be kicked from the nest.

This can manifest in the child growing up and continually raising the bar on what they think will be deemed good enough. They need to get great results in school and usually do because they strive harder and harder. But the result is that parents now know they have a successful child. They don't want to spoil the child, so they don't make a huge deal of it all the time. The child still doesn't get the accolades they need to hear, and the issue is exaggerated.

Roll on to adulthood. This person now pushes themselves harder, continually raising the bar of excellence. We get perfectionism, anxiety and unrelenting standards that must be attained, often at crippling levels. And the cycle continues.

Does this sound familiar at all? If so, welcome to a very large club.

Clinical anxiety

I want to touch on clinical anxiety briefly to explain what a doctor would need to see before diagnosing someone with anxiety. Without getting too far into it, the person needs to be experiencing symptoms on 'more days than not' over a six-month period.

There are seven generally recognised types of anxiety in the diagnostic field. This book is about self-care, so we don't need to examine the differences and criteria behind each trait. But for this exercise, let's assume we are considering the sub-clinical circumstances.

These are what most people experience as some form of non-specific, generalised anxiety that is enough to interfere in their lives or their days temporarily. If your anxiety is greater than that, please keep reading but consider seeking primary health care support. Anxiety doesn't go away by itself; we need to work at it.

As with most conditions, anxiety is seen today through the biopsychosocial model. If that seems like lazy cobbling together of three words, you're right. It really is that.

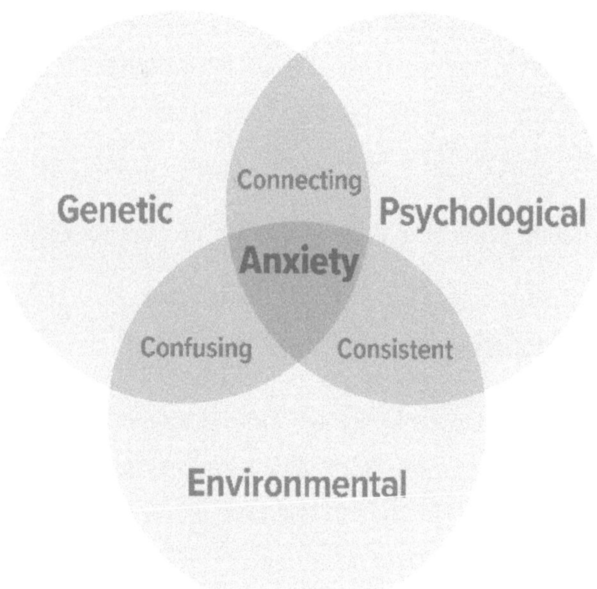

Figure 4: Components of anxiety

There is a biological element to anxiety. The jury is still out on whether there are specific DNA markers, but there does seem to be a genetic component, as anxiety appears to be hereditary. Alongside the biological factor, we must also have some psychological factors, such as perfectionism or consistent worry, and an element of social triggers like high stress levels to kick the whole thing off. The issue is created through a complex interaction between the three components.

Of course, not all anxiety meets these criteria.

But that does not, to my mind, diminish its effect and how it can interfere massively in someone's life. So, we describe sub-clinical presentations, elevated states and traits of anxiety, or anxiety-related distress. These can be challenging to manage and impact how we should support ourselves when we experience them.

That is the *what* of anxiety. Let's talk about *how* we deal with it. And it isn't all bad because the prevention steps are good for our overall self-care and wellbeing.

In previous chapters, we discussed ways to support wellbeing that also help with self-care.

> *The primary action is to regulate breathing.*

The primary action is to regulate breathing, which tells the autonomic nervous system (ANS) that we are not in danger when triggered into a fight or flight response. The ANS does not know the difference between anger, anxiety or stress and will respond in a way that says, 'I am under attack and need to be prepared'.

So, our systems kick into safety mode, the breath often quickens, and we may perspire. We focus on one thing, get that slightly sick feeling in our stomachs, and start to tremble. Hormones are now coursing through our bodies to prepare us for what it is anticipating.

That usually happens outside our awareness and occurs in what Dr Caroline Leaf calls the nonconscious mind.[3] Coming from memory stores deeply rooted in the nonconscious mind, it triggers an emotional and physical response in the subconscious (where our ANS is, like a watchdog ready to spring into action). Then the conscious mind, our thought process, responds and manifests in words and considered actions.

In his book, *The Body Keeps The Score*, Bessel van der Kolk says trauma and anxiety live in the body, not just in the memory banks.[4]

Our response is often felt there, without having a thought process to work with.

The underlying message is that everything is working as it is designed to. Our ANS has kept us alive thus far, and, as a species, we have managed to evolve pretty well. This system and its process are our friends. We should not deny it or avoid it. We can embrace it and thank it for a job well done so far. Now, we just need to control it a little better.

Rather than being overwhelmed, we can learn to step aside and become our own paramedics. We can deal with the symptoms we are experiencing and prevent other symptoms from overwhelming us, treating the presenting symptoms as a paramedic would.

We can develop enough composure to ensure we are no longer in response mode, removing us from the danger response zone.

My strategies for managing anxiety

A helpful tool is a well-established management theory called the SWOT Analysis. This tool can help to guide our actions and response in the face of uncertainty and indecision when we are unsure how to react to our anxious situation. We can explore our Strengths and Weaknesses for internal support. Then we can review any external Opportunities to do things differently and identify any Threats to our safety.

This tool can be especially helpful in considering the likely outcomes of decisions, choices and actions. Another useful way of determining each element is to list the things we can control and the things we can't, then focus energy only on what we can influence.

Try this and see if you can map a strategy or process for when you may need it. This exercise is best practised when you are not in a heightened state of anxiety, as your responses may be too emotional. In any event, use it as a preparation strategy.

Figure 5: SWOT strategies

Mammalian diving reflex

Humans evolved with a primitive reflex designed to prevent us from drowning. It's called the mammalian diving reflex and shows as we instinctively hold our breath underwater. That's why we feel safe teaching kids to be comfortable in the water from a very young age.

When your face is submerged in cold water, your body immediately kicks in a part of the nervous system that slows everything down. Try this method if you are feeling panic, intense overwhelm or anxiety.

Fill a sink or bowl with cold water. The colder, the better.

Submerge your face for fifteen seconds. If you can't, just a quick dip or splash your face. A wet towel won't do the job.

Repeat if you need to.

Breathing

We could fill another book on the various methods of controlling and regulating breathing. There are many excellent techniques. Some simple exercises include diaphragm breathing, where you place your hands on your tummy, or solar plexus, noticing it moving up and down with the breath. Allow your belly to expand with a full, deep and slow breath in and out.

Another way of experiencing that full range of breath into your lungs is to try 'breathing into the back', where you use a chair, your (or someone else's) hands to gauge and guide your breath.

Opening and closing your hands with the in-and-out movement of the breath is another centring and grounding exercise. It brings attention to the present moment as you clench and unclench your hands. This simple practice can be done anywhere.

Many websites and apps offer guided breath meditations. They are a superb source of support and calmness when we need them. Download them to your smartphone, so they are at hand when you need them. My preferred apps are Calm, Headspace and Balance. Find what works for you.

> *Find what works for you.*

Box breathing

I think box breathing is my personal favourite.

To practice this, you follow a specific, controlled pattern. Breathe in for four seconds. Hold your breath for four seconds. Breathe out for four seconds. And hold again for four seconds. Then repeat.

Ready to try it? Now, try going through the sequence four times, which ends up being just over a minute.

I like to practice this whenever I am in the water, especially if I am underwater for the breathe-out part. It is astonishing how the body reacts to being underwater without air in the lungs!

Every police and military response group around the world uses this strategy to regain composure and regulate anxiety under challenging situations. Even Olympic athletes practice box breathing just before competing, especially in shooting and archery sports.

Rising anxiety is the body preparing for a situation.

Rising anxiety is the body preparing for a situation.

5-4-3-2-1

Yet another grounding exercise is known as 5-4-3-2-1. You can do this yourself or guide someone else through it. This can help them to regulate, even in a panic attack. Try introducing it to kids as a game, so they can experience what it is like. It is especially useful for anxious kids.

First, ask the person (or yourself) to describe five things you can see. Not just look at them; you need to name them out loud. This ensures anchoring in the here-and-now.

Next, name four things you can feel or touch. Three things you can hear. Two things you can smell and one thing you can taste.

Here's an example.

Five things you can see: another person, a table, a clock on the wall, the cat and a tree outside the window.

Four things you can feel/touch: the table, my shirt, a pen and a book.

Three things you can hear: the clock ticking, people talking and traffic.

Two things you can smell: food and flowers.

One thing you can taste: coffee.

A slightly different ending can be to name one good thing about yourself. Something that you are proud of or for which you are grateful.

This last one is particularly clever as your brain cannot think anxious thoughts and gratitude at the same time.

The sequence you decide on doesn't matter. It doesn't even matter if you cannot find everything.

The practice of looking around and naming things grounds you in the present moment, which is all you are trying to achieve.

Short meditation

This is one of my favourites and something I do before every online meeting or training session. This meditation gatha (poem) was written by Thich Nhat Hanh, a renowned Zen monk who was instrumental in bringing mindfulness to Western society.

The meditation involves four breaths in and four out, slowly and rhythmically. When doing so, you silently say the words as follows:

> In, Out
>
> Deep, Slow

Calm, Ease

Smile, Release

Each breath is an indicator or pointer to a part of the practice. As Thich Nhat Hanh said, 'Breathing in, I am aware of breathing in. Breathing out, I am aware of breathing out. I let go of everything else and focus my attention on the physical act of the breath. But all I have to say is In, out.'[5]

When you are new to the practice, each word is enough to keep your attention focused. As you progress, you don't need to utter the word (although I still do, as I like it) and can simply focus on your breath.

The breath becomes slower and regulated; this is where *Deep, Slow* comes in. Use it to remind yourself to deepen and slow your breath.

Calm, Ease reminds you of the mental state that you desire. Check where you are holding any tension in the body or where gratitude is directing your attention.

Smile, Release lightens and gives you permission to acknowledge and name any anxious feelings or thoughts, and let them go, release them.

Acceptance and Commitment Therapy (ACT)

Acceptance and commitment therapy (ACT) is a relatively new and valuable treatment method for anxiety regulation. It relies on helping people behave more consistently with their values rather than focusing on any deficit (something wrong). We can then apply mindfulness and acceptance skills to our reactions and responses to uncontrollable or anxiety-ridden experiences.

ACT therapy is less concerned with eliminating unwanted thoughts, emotions and sensations. It is much more about cultivating psychological flexibility.

The ACT model predicts that people will be most effective when they can:

- Accept automatic thoughts, sensations and urges.
- De-fuse from thinking (i.e., observe thoughts without believing them or following their directions).
- Attend to the present moment with self-awareness (more on this in a coming chapter).
- Clearly articulate boundaries (i.e., self-directed, desirable ways of behaving).
- Engage in committed action (i.e., participating in activities consistent with boundaries, even when psychologically challenging).

> *We aren't wrong or broken.*

I like the ACT model because of its fresh approach to the idea that we aren't wrong or broken. Life is what it is, and we can deal with it. This goes a long way to reducing stigma, self-stigma, perceived slights and self-recrimination.

Cognitive fusion and de-fusion

Steven C. Hayes is the American psychologist who developed ACT. He introduced the term *cognitive fusion* to illustrate times when we are so tightly stuck in our thoughts and beliefs we become fused with them.

When experiencing cognitive fusion, we can't separate ourselves from our thoughts. Our thoughts become our reality. To put it crudely, we believe our own bullshit. We feel disconnected from the world outside our thoughts, removed from our senses, what we're doing, and even the people around us.

The opposite of cognitive fusion is cognitive de-fusion. This involves stepping back from what's going on in our minds and detaching from our thoughts. It takes practice but is very doable.

In this state of de-fusion, we can observe our thoughts and other internal sensations, emotions, feelings and processes without getting lost, stuck or fused with them. We can learn to simply notice our thoughts, watch them, accept them and let them go if we choose to.

An example is where we might feel less-than for some reason. We might say, 'I'm stupid'. Rather than taking that on and swallowing it whole, as usual, we can say to ourselves, 'I notice that I am having that thought again. I wonder where it is coming from?'

We can now explore the sequence of events that led us to this erroneous conclusion and correct it.

We can adopt many tactics and strategies to challenge and overcome our anxiety. I am a great fan of acknowledging that anxiety exists, confronting it and exploring its effects. We don't need to befriend anxiety, but we should not avoid it.

Above all else, avoid avoiding anxiety

Above all else, avoid avoiding anxiety

This approach is known as Step back, stand down, sit down. I learned it from Zjamal Xanitha, a friend, fellow psychotherapist and lecturer whom I greatly admire.[6]

If you experience some anxiety, the process is as follows.

Step back

Observe the event or situation, its concrete, specific details, and accept the reality of the current situation.

For example, when anxiety is trying to dominate my mind, it usually wants me to fight or escape. But I choose a different response, saying 'I can handle this situation'.

Stand down (soften down)

It is well documented that physical touch, even our own, is instrumental in triggering the parasympathetic response and calming us down. We can use our hands on our bodies to soothe our ANS response, giving ourselves a hug or a pat on the arm.

The next thing to say is, 'This is not an emergency'. If I start to think it is, my body will begin to help me out by taking me into hyper-arousal.

So, we allow our anxiety to be here with us.

Sit down

Calming breaths are in order here too, as with any response to anxiety or state of distress.

The skill to develop is embracing doubt and distress. Just as you would if you wanted to calm an upset child. You certainly wouldn't give a voice to your inner critic.

You need to be with it as if you're saying, 'I want this experience'. Doing so reduces its power and grip. I liken it to standing up to a bully, as we find the fear dissipates and can tolerate the discomfort. From then on, that particular trigger is reduced.

Settle yourself

You're often just a few slow breaths from feeling calm.

Try these breathing and calming exercises, and you will find you are never far from settling yourself. You're often just a few slow breaths from feeling calm. Most of the time, we can bring ourselves down safely and easily from that heightened state of anxiety by settling our ANS response. It just takes a little getting used to and the habit of self-care practice.

Our bodies are exquisitely designed to seek balance when we allow the right conditions to prevail.

It doesn't want to be in a state of flux between stress and distress.

Homeostasis is the process whereby we move towards a place of balance. It is the condition of optimal functioning, and we are designed to move towards it if we allow it. The best way to do that is to create the conditions and environment where we can flourish. And when we stray from that path, we return using our internal resources.

There is an old saying of unknown origin: 'through the body is the way'. As we've shared, there is more than just what presents itself or seems obvious. Self-care is a holistic, whole-of-person approach that involves all of us. Perhaps that is most obvious when understanding anxiety and how it manifests. I trust the information in this chapter has given you fresh insight into what it is and what you can do about it. Go gently.

PART TWO

LOOK IN

CHAPTER FOUR

Get Back on Track with a Healthy Brain

'He who looks outside dreams, who looks inside, awakes'

— Carl Jung

PART TWO: LOOK IN

Questions: Did you remember to eat breakfast this morning? Are you drinking enough water? Do you take time out for yourself? What do you do to play?

In this chapter, we look inwards. It's important.

Most people don't realise that mental health exists on a spectrum, just like physical health.

> *Mental health exists on a spectrum.*

Imagine a scale of one to ten. You could probably point to where you believe your physical health lies. You probably also have an opinion on whether it could be improved or if you are happy to maintain where you are.

Physical health level doesn't change dramatically or quickly unless something adverse occurs. We get sick or injured and catch a bad flu or Covid, that floors us for a while, and then we recover. We take steps to care for ourselves, ease the journey and feel better.

However, mental health is often seen as something that is or isn't present — as if a switch turns it on or off. Nothing could be further from the truth. We can have good mental health, and we can have challenged or poor mental health. It lives on the same scale or spectrum as physical health.

I confess that I have long recognised the value of mindfulness and meditation, but I didn't practice either until relatively recently. I'm happy to have finally made them part of my self-care practice. Ironically, if people who knew me years ago heard that I meditate, they'd have to be picked up off the floor from laughing.

I am not exactly sure what finally compelled me to try mindfulness and meditation. My stress or anxiety levels may have increased to the point where my sleep was interrupted. Or perhaps I found myself too busy to take a regular break. Or I felt guilty that I could be doing more if I didn't take a break. But I do know that I have often witnessed people in our treatment facilities finding peace and grounding from trying these techniques.

In one organisation, the clinicians meditated together for five to ten minutes before they began their shift. It was an incredible experience as it meant that everyone in the team started with the same grounded and calm mindset. A collective peace permeated the building, and the residents (I dislike the term patient) would experience this and be assured of their safety. Maybe this is where it merged into my practice.

Can you imagine every team in your organisation beginning their day with a grounding practice?

I use a Tibetan singing bowl as my grounding tool. I love focusing on the peaceful sound as a single tap quietly fades away.

Whatever the trigger that began my meditation practice, I wouldn't be without it now, as simple practices take little time, and the payback is enormous.

Simple practices take little time.

This chapter will examine what we can use to relax, focus on what's important to us, and reflect on what we want. For example, we often talk about taking *time out* for ourselves but rarely about taking *time in*. Both are equally important.

In the last chapter, we discussed the importance of remembering to eat and drink water during the day. That's because a healthy gut biome supports the mood-stabilising hormones the brain needs to carry us through protracted periods of stress.

Here we'll look at how the precursors to burnout relate to self-care by looking inwards.

The threat response

You'll remember that when the autonomic nervous system and fight or flight response are activated, it does not recognise the difference between danger and stress. It is aware we are under some sort of attack or distress and responds — whether or not the perceived threat is real.

Our reactions are carefully orchestrated and almost instantaneous, producing hormonal responses and physiological reactions to help us. Blood is re-directed from internal organs to the extremities to ready us for action. Our vision tightens, and we lose peripheral vision. Our breathing quickens. We begin to sweat to cool down and tremble as adrenaline and cortisol course through our bloodstream and muscles.

If any of this sounds familiar, it may be because of stress rather than danger. You may notice these are also responses to anxiety and anxious thought patterns. I see value in going into detail in this description as it relates to so much of our self-care.

Understanding the threat process can alleviate the feelings of anxiety that so many people struggle with. Recognising the physical responses goes a long way to removing the mystery surrounding anxiety and anxious thoughts. It also explains the harm caused to almost every organ in the body if we don't tend to our stress levels. When we know what is happening, we can take steps to alleviate the harm and reduce our exposure to the effects.

To understand what's going on, we must look at the structure of the brain.

You may be surprised to learn that we do *not* have three parts to the brain, as figure 6 suggests. The three-part brain is more a descriptor than a biological reality. We know that evolution has determined differing reactions to the stress response, but we don't actually have a lizard brain. Even if it isn't factual, I believe it is a helpful analogy, so I continue to use it.

If you want to delve deeper into this topic, I recommend Professor Kerryn Phelps' superb book *How to Keep Your Brain Young*.[1]

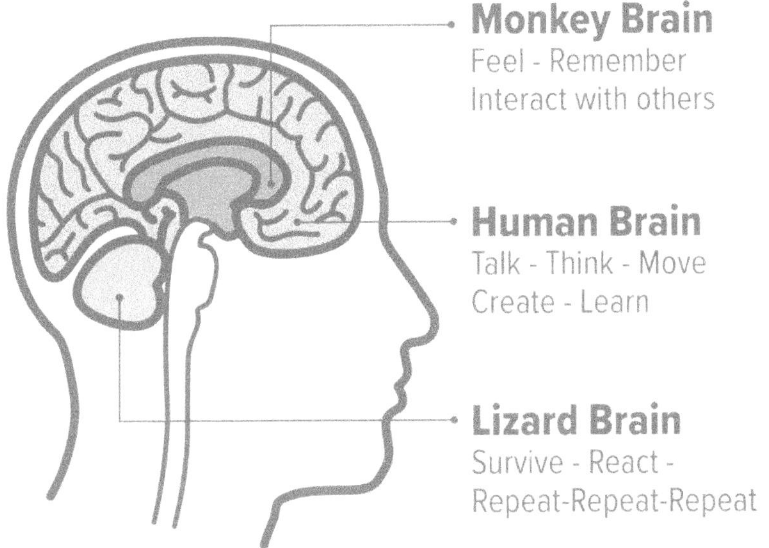

Figure 6: Three parts of the brain

Here is what is occurring in the brain.

The middle part of the brain (labelled the Monkey Brain in figure 6) is where all sensory information is received. The amygdala is part of the limbic system. This is the brain's watchdog and traffic lights. Information comes in and is processed, and the amygdala determines where the information goes.

If it doesn't sense danger, the information goes to the Human Brain (the frontal cortex or thinking brain) for action.

If it does sense danger, it will direct the information through the hypothalamus, or command centre, and on to the reptilian or Lizard Brain. Its primary function is to be involved in the things necessary for survival. These are the things we don't generally think about or control, such as body temperature, balance, breathing, blinking and other automatic responses.

This primary brain function is the mechanism that activates our physical response to harm. This function activates our need to flee, fight or freeze. Several other responses (such as folding or fawning) can occur, but these three 'brain parts' are the primary responses in this self-care exercise. The Lizard Brain works faster than if we tried to figure it out in our thinking brain or frontal cortex, meaning we can respond without thinking if we feel in danger or distress. It is what has kept the human species evolving.

The process involves the nervous system, specifically the autonomic nervous system (ANS). And for this exercise, we are interested in two sections that operate in harmony with each other, called the sympathetic and parasympathetic nervous systems. (I remember the difference between the two as the sympathetic NS activates in sympathy with our stress response, while the parasympathetic NS is like the 'paramedic' that comes along to relieve it.)

The sympathetic nervous system (SNS) is like the accelerator in a car, a short-term response that bursts into action — the fight or flight response. The parasympathetic nervous system (PNS) is like the brake. It slows down and reduces the effects of the accelerator. Known as rest and digest, it is a longer-term response when we reverse the effects of the first reaction.

As humans evolved, we spent shorter periods in fight or flight and longer in rest and digest mode. Exactly as we should.

Today, however, modern lifestyles mean we spend inordinate amounts of time on the first reaction. As discussed earlier, our brain doesn't know the difference between stress and danger and reacts anyway.

We walk ten per cent faster than even a decade ago, and this increase seems to be a recurring pattern. We live in urban areas where noise has tripled in the last twenty-five years.[2] Everything from our morning alarm, emails pinging, traffic noise, phones ringing, and all the other sudden noises trigger the acoustic startle response and fires up the fight or flight system.

It is not good.

We spend far too much time in fight or flight and not nearly enough in rest and digest.

Redressing the balance

Thanks for hanging in there. We need to know why we must focus on reducing fight or flight and increasing rest and digest. Our lives and health systems depend on it.

> *We must focus on reducing fight or flight.*

So, what can we do?

Taking care of brain health is a hugely important part of self-care. With proper care, we can reduce or clear grogginess, enhance memory and boost cognitive function (think better).

In the first chapter, we covered the physical elements of self-care. There is undoubtedly a cross-over between physical and brain or mental health. Let's explore some approaches you can take to support your ability to improve your brain's health.

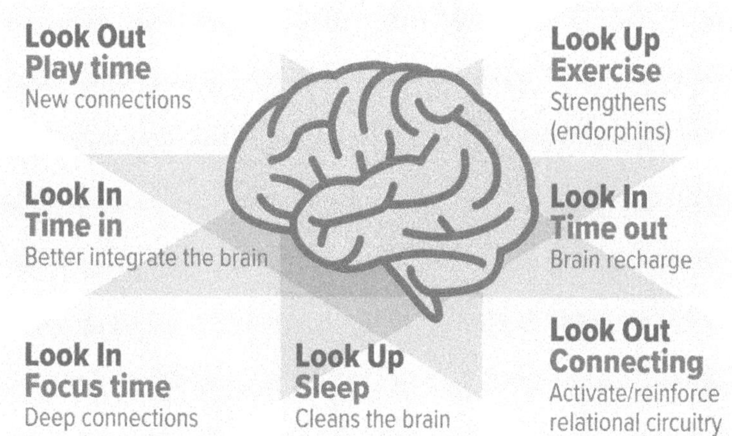

Figure 7: Approaches to supporting brain health

This part of our conversation is a nod to the work of Dr Dan Siegel and The Healthy Mind Platter.[3] The brain is far more than just a super-computer. It is a living, breathing organ. The diagram in figure 7 explains some of the elements related to the brain.

Exercise: 'On yer bike'

In June 2022, Time Magazine published an article showing how people's motivation to exercise has shifted dramatically. It is no longer around controlling weight and looking good; the primary reasons for exercising today are reducing stress and anxiety, improving sleep, and feeling better mentally.

I get something really positive from my two-to-three-times-a-week spin (cycling) classes. Invigorating exercise that isn't focused on body image works for me. My body image ship has well and truly sailed. Spin class is the one place where I can swear freely. The running joke is that I am the only one allowed to swear during class (something to do with my Irish accent making it seem almost pleasant!). Recently my smart watch flashed me a message during class, saying, 'You don't have a Jesus Christ in your contacts. Who are you trying to call?' I was gutted that I wasn't fast enough to take a screen shot!

Where mental wellbeing was once a happy side-effect of chasing the six-pack or torching calories, now it is the whole point. I love that this shift has come about in improving our mindsets. It's less about punishing exercise routines and more about recovery and repair work.

Since the days of Jane Fonda telling us to 'go for the burn and work it', we've known about the mood-boosting runner's high, where endorphins are released from exercising.

We know that exercise increases our heart rate, pumping oxygen to the brain so it can do its thing. But there is other stuff going on as well.

Besides the endorphins, brain-derived neurotropic factor (BDNF) is like a natural steroid. It is involved in learning and absorbing information, improving long-term memory, strengthening the brain and promoting neurogenesis, or new brain cells, and enhancing mental abilities. All this at the same time as acting against anxiety, stress and depression. Hugely important.

So regular exercise isn't about body image; it does so much to support our brains to be as healthy as every other organ. We can hurt it, or we can help it. It's up to us.

Regular exercise isn't about body image.

Time out: Counting your toes

I describe *time out* as an opportunity to let the mind wander. Trying to focus attention on something for too long or too often can be harmful, and it's undoubtedly exhausting. So, just like a muscle, it is okay to let the mind just relax and flop.

Of course, there is a time and place for it. If you continually wander to negative thoughts, perhaps you need to seek support. And try not to mind-wander when you are meant to concentrate, like driving or in an important meeting.

Instead, set aside time each day to sit still in a quiet place and watch what happens.

Time out can often help solve a niggling problem or issue. You can reach a conclusion that has eluded you, manage conflict and reduce anxiety. It can boost productivity and improve problem-solving skills necessary for increasing resilience and motivation. And most importantly, it can help you decide on, and achieve, your goals.

Time out recharges the brain by increasing alpha brain waves in the prefrontal cortex. That is good as it simultaneously exercises and relaxes the brain. It also releases dopamine, a neurotransmitter essential for mood-regulating and feeling rewarded and satisfied.

Connecting and belonging to our tribe

I mentioned earlier that Bessel van der Kolk says that feeling safe in the company of others is the single most crucial aspect of good mental health. To feel safe where we feel we belong. It's important here too.

Brené Brown takes this even further. She says that fitting in is about assessing a situation and becoming who you need to be, to be accepted. That is a safety move. As she writes, 'Belonging ... doesn't require us to change who we are; it requires us to be who we are'.[4] There is a big difference between fitting in and belonging. And it comes down to the motivation to connect and feel safe.

> *There is a big difference between fitting in and belonging.*

We are social creatures, pack animals. When we feel more connected, we have lower stress, anxiety and depression levels. In the right company, we learn to regulate our emotions and develop higher levels of self-esteem.

Loneliness and isolation are fast becoming some of the most significant issues in society. Some research likens the health harm of loneliness to smoking fifteen cigarettes a day. We are living longer, which often means losing life-long friends and partners. We experience disconnection and are working remotely. Don't rush to blame social media, as that can be positive and negative in supporting connections. How we use it is up to us.

Healthy connections and doing all we can to reduce isolation by engaging in activities that connect us to family and friends are vital. Dancing, singing, exercising, hobbies, or any other way of connecting with people whose company we enjoy, pays big dividends. As my dear mother used to say, 'Who would choose to be lonely?'

In terms of brain health, connecting with others releases serotonin and dopamine, the two mood hormones. Endorphins are released, and oxytocin is released, creating feelings of trust and bonding.

Sleep

We discussed the importance of sleep in Chapter One, but I want to reiterate that scientists are discovering links to Alzheimer's disease and sleep deprivation from lifestyle choices and poor sleep hygiene. Irregular bedtimes, alcohol intake, exercise, chronic stress and insomnia, intermittent fasting, and omega-three consumption can all affect the glymphatic system and its work.

Irregular bedtimes tell the brain that we must stay awake, assuming we must be in danger. Melatonin production stops, making it harder to get to sleep. Then cortisol production is interrupted, so waking up with energy is lost to us. Mounting evidence also shows a relationship between mood disorders and poor sleep. We used to think the brain rested when we slept. Now we know it is very active indeed.

I hope this information motivates you to develop better sleep hygiene and behaviour. Good brain health depends on it.

Focus time

I need you to focus on focusing.

Research has shed light on the power of focus and its role as a driver of success. This ability to focus forms deep connections in our brain and, in effect, makes it stronger and more efficient. We can only concentrate for fifty to ninety-minute periods for about four hours a day. Air-traffic controllers are a good example as they can only do this work for short periods.

Even our emotional state affects our ability to give something the attention it needs.

Yet as helpful as focusing can be, it has a downside.

Excessive focus can exhaust the focus circuits in the brain. It can drain energy, make us lose self-control, impair decision-making, and make us less collaborative. This is another way of saying that too much focus can make you cranky.

Simple techniques pay enormous dividends. To-do lists can help us stay on track. A ten-minute meditation break helps. Or try the Pomodoro method, which involves twenty-five minutes of work, and then a five-minute break. After four blocks, take an extended break. Try eating your lunch in silence and with your eyes closed, concentrating on your food. It's an amazing sensation!

Taking breaks when we should (or when we feel like we need them) ultimately strengthens our brain connections, incorporating many different areas of the brain and streamlining its ability to function at its best.

Time in

Time in is about investing in quality time to be quietly reflective. It is an ideal time to meditate, perhaps. This is slightly different from focusing, which we just discussed. This type of meditation focuses on the sensations you are experiencing. It's not about trying to make sense of them, just notice what you are emotionally feeling right now and where you feel the sensation in the body. It involves exploring feelings and emotions without the deep concentration of a targeted meditation.

Switching from deep focus to letting the mind wander engages a brain circuit called the default mode network. This network activates old memories, rolling back and forth between the past, present and future and recombining different ideas.

This time helps integrate different areas in the brain, exercising the various connections and how they cooperate. It's like clearing away the cobwebs so the brain traffic can flow more freely.

Silence helps enormously — if you can find it. Even a few minutes every day. It's not as easy as it sounds (if you'll pardon the pun). So, grab silence when you can, but don't tell anyone, or they may ruin it for you. Silence can help increase self-awareness and self-compassion and allow us to become more mindful. Beautiful work in improving brain health.

Play time

George Bernard Shaw famously said we don't stop playing because we grow old. We grow old because we stop playing. It is never too late to get back to having fun and introducing some playtime into our lives. There's nothing like a good belly laugh to make us feel good.

We grow old because we stop playing.

This excerpt from an article on the importance of play offers possibly the best definition I have come across.

> 'Play could be simply goofing off with friends, sharing jokes with a coworker, throwing a frisbee on the beach, dressing up on Halloween with your kids, building a snowman in the yard, playing fetch with a dog, acting out charades at a party, or going for a bike ride with your spouse with no destination in mind. There doesn't need to be any point to the activity beyond having fun and enjoying yourself. By permitting yourself to play with the joyful abandon of childhood, you can reap oodles of health benefits throughout life.'[5]

Play manifests in the brain by creating new connections between different areas. It increases the size of the prefrontal cortex, meaning that the brain is more efficient at making plans, solving problems, and regulating and identifying emotions, all things required for successful social interactions. Play enhances emotional intelligence, boosts self-esteem, and deepens connections with others. It's highly beneficial for good brain health.

What's not to like about that?

Your activities can support and harm your brain, just like any other organ in the body. Some things promote good brain health, while others cause measurable damage.

We know that adults with higher playfulness have less perceived stress. And we only need to look at a child using their imagination to understand what play looks like.

Adults with higher playfulness have less perceived stress.

There are many ways to develop both grey and white brain matter for a stronger, fitter brain. It's just like muscles and exercise.

And, just like any muscle, we need to give it a break from time to time. Even a short rest can make a massive difference to your mindset. There are plenty of advantages to brief ten or twenty-minute breaks or even an hour. And, of course, several hours during sleep.

Let's consider how to take these breaks.

One-minute break

Just take one minute to close your eyes and breathe deeply and slowly. That's it.

Five-minute break: Pomodoro technique

The Pomodoro technique is one of the better ways to counter the idea that taking breaks is a time-waster. Developed as a time management tool by Francesco Cirillo in the late 1980s, the technique uses a timer to break work into intervals, traditionally twenty-five minutes in length, separated by short breaks of five minutes. After four rounds, take a more extended break.

I use Siri to set the alarm on my phone for twenty-five minutes, then reset it each time. Plenty of apps can manage this part of the exercise for you.

What do you do with your five-minute break? I try to get out in the sun or fresh air for a few minutes in at least one of the breaks. Or make a cup of tea. Or try a breathing exercise.

Or find a silent space somewhere near you. This needs complete silence and is a really valuable meditation exercise. Such silence is also far easier to say than to find. Honestly, when was the last time you experienced complete silence in a conscious state? It will be hugely valuable if you can.

Twenty-minute break

Ernest Lawrence Rossi quotes research that indicates we need to take a break every 90-120 minutes, especially when our bodies tell us to.[6] While there is conflicting evidence around the science Rossi uses, there is undoubtedly consensus around the need for regular breaks.

It is suggested that a twenty-minute break can deliver increased concentration, improved performance, and deeper concentration for up to two hours after the break. When speaking with groups, I use the analogy of a break offering 5:1 return. It is such a 'sure thing' that we should never turn our back on such an investment.

A famous Zen saying advises that you should sit in nature for twenty minutes a day, unless you're busy, in which case you should sit for an hour.

In the previous chapter, we discussed the value of meditating for ten to fifteen minutes in the morning and before going to sleep. Doing this is particularly valuable if you wake up ruminating in the middle of the night. If you can meditate then, you are ideally placed to meditate for twenty minutes during the day to take a break when needed.

There are plenty of breathing exercises, meditations (stationary or moving) or exercises you can perform in twenty minutes. Insight Timer is an app that is freely available on phones with a wide range of meditations you can try before you buy. As I've said, I have a yearning for Tibetan singing bowls and pranayama (breathing exercises and meditations).

In twenty minutes, you can take a brisk walk, spend it focusing and take some time in or time out. Focus on any element of brain health during this time of rest.

CHAPTER FIVE

Float With the Tide

You may have noticed that the questions usually seen at the beginning of the chapter are missing. This time they are within the chapter, at the end of each of the six domains of resilience.

Resilience is a fascinating topic. But, like stress programs from twenty years ago, it seems to have adopted a reputation it does not deserve.

I sometimes run into resistance or reluctance from teams within organisations where they have concluded that the only reason the company puts them through resilience coaching or training is to squeeze even more effort from them. A bit like a toothpaste tube nearing the end.

Resilience is most definitely a self-care process.

I have a different slant on this. To my mind, resilience is most definitely a self-care process. And indeed, the resilience coaching I deliver is focused on the individual. Admittedly, we explore (as we will here) elements of resilience that speak to how we collaborate and inter-relate with others in our team or community. Still, ultimately it is about the 'self'.

There will likely be some positives for the organisation in that a team member with greater resilience and buoyancy will be more deeply engaged in their work. They will likely connect better, work more productively and develop sustainable performance. But that is a happy coincidence rather than the aim of the game. The real purpose of developing and increasing resilience is to find the positive and take advantage of what occurs for us. To find opportunity in adversity and emerge with that advantage.

Resilience means having a skillset that supports our self-care and balance. My focus is on six elements of resilience that are based on the extensive research and work of Jurie G. Rossouw and his colleagues.[1] These elements are illustrated in figure 8.

Figure 8: Six domains of resilience

Defining the terms

When I speak about balance, I mean that state of equilibrium we all seek where we are self-supporting and living in a healthy and fruitful way. When we are out of balance, we usually try to soothe ourselves or try to rectify the situation and return to balance.

Just as it is said that health is much more than the absence of illness, resilience is far more than the absence of stress. People will usually tell you that resilience is about bouncing back from stressful experiences or returning from adversity.

Resilience is far more than the absence of stress.

In medicine and psychology, the premise is often to look at the disease model, focusing on the deficit or negative. In other words, when thinking about resilience, we could look at stressful experiences through the lens of what's wrong. The effort is in returning to zero or a mid-level/neutral point, and correcting the imbalance.

On the other hand, positive psychology looks at strengths and uses them to pull the person through by looking for what's right.

A good metaphor for this process is the idea of buoyancy or floating rather than sinking.

But being ready and prepared for adversity is only half the story. Finding opportunity in adversity and responding positively, or capitalising, gives us the edge.

That's the definition of resilience I prefer to use: Resilience is the ability to respond positively to adversity.

For example, if you go to the gym and do the usual ten squats and ten push-ups, you respond to the stress you put on your body and recover from the applied stress. But what happens when you need to respond to a significant and unexpected stress level? You may not have the resources to respond positively.

But if you increase your ten push-ups and ten squats to a level that challenges you a little more, you adapt and are prepared. You can respond accordingly when the need arises.

As a side note, remember that rest is where the true effort from the gym work is corralled. Unless you rest during times of stress, the gains begin to diminish.

The point is that focusing on the following six domains of resilience improves self-awareness, self-care and self-growth. By happy coincidence, these also serve us to become more deeply engaged and with sustainable performance throughout all our lives.

Health

What are your sleep, diet, exercise and mindset levels like? We covered these in earlier chapters, but keep them in mind now too. Health is a foundational domain of resilience. Various studies have shown how much physical health can impact wellbeing simply because it strongly affects our experience of life.

That's especially so when everything is not working as it should.

For example, Silverman and Deuster's research[2] suggested that the processes where physical health promotes increased resilience and wellbeing and the relationships between positive psychological and physical health are diverse and complex. They confirmed that 'physical fitness appears to buffer against stress-related disease owing to its blunting/optimising effects on hormonal stress-responsive systems, such as the hypothalamic-pituitary-adrenal axis and the sympathetic nervous system'.

Basically, they're saying that our fight or flight response is regulated when we are physically healthy.

In the short term, we think faster and more accurately, with fewer brain fog issues. According to some research, our nerve-growth brain-derived neurotropic factor (BDNF) acts as a natural steroid when we are active, and supports neurogenesis, or simply the growth and replacement of brain cells.[3]

In the longer term, this protects against disease and supports neural efficiency and increased brain connectivity.

So, in considering your resilience levels, ask yourself the following questions. What is my current state of physical health like? Do I exercise regularly? Am I eating healthily? Do I get quality and restful sleep? What's my overall sense of health and wellbeing? Do I know how to look after myself? What's my level of health? Am I satisfied with it, or do I want to improve it?

These fundamental questions around resilience need to be the basis for everything else we do.

Vision

If health is the foundation of resilience, then vision is probably the most critical domain.

Vision talks about our sense of purpose and what drives us. In many respects, it shows us our direction in life. This includes our vision for how we aspire to be as individuals and how we prefer to be seen and perceived.

> *Vision is like a car's GPS navigation system.*

Vision is like a car's GPS navigation system choosing the best course.

A clear vision gives us confidence that we can achieve the bold goals we set. That's particularly so if we share our vision with those closest to us. Goals are essential to motivating and staying on the path.

Vision and goals also clarify priorities and guide decisions. A sense of self-worth and personal ability flows from this sense of assuredness.

Of course, I speak of vision and goal setting in the context of ourselves, our self-purpose and self-worth. They can also be intertwined with the purpose and vision of our team or organisation at work. The two sets of purpose don't have to align precisely, but it helps if they don't clash.

It could even be said that we can share a vision of perceived dangers we may face as a team at work, which isn't as high an ideal as sharing a vision of prosperity and growth. But it may be equally as important when it comes to collective resilience or congruence.

Thad Allen, a former admiral in the US Coast Guard, said in a 2012 speech, 'When there is a shared vision of the mission, commitment to the shared values of an organisation and strong and effective leadership that enables employees to be successful, morale happens.'[4]

Research suggests that having identifiable goals supports us in exploring and considering alternatives to test our vision from time to time.

Don't worry about perfectionism (it doesn't exist). Stay true to your values, goals and all that you hold dear.

Trust your judgement and your gut instinct (it is almost always right), but anticipate problems, expect mistakes, find lessons or opportunities and bounce back.

Trust your judgement.

Perfection is not the end goal in pursuing a vision, so don't worry about it. Stay true to your values and principles and trust your judgement. The real key to resilience is being able to bounce back from those mistakes. Change direction, correct the mistake and move on. That's how we find opportunity in adversity.

If you wish to explore your resilience level in the context of vision, ask yourself the following questions:

Do I have a sense of purpose and meaning in my life? Outside of work as well as career aspirations?

Do I feel I am in control and have choices around my destiny, goals, ambitions and vision?

How can I improve my vision and clarity of purpose? Can I define my goals and explain them easily to others?

One final great question to ask is this. Can I change my goals if my direction or circumstances shift?

We must allow ourselves the space to research and consider alternatives if we need to.

Composure

The third element of resilience is composure. Can we drive slow and steady, staying in our lane, or are we lane-hopping and getting frustrated?

As an entity of resilience, composure speaks to how effectively we can stay calm and regulate or control our emotional response to adversity. We'll talk more about emotional intelligence in Chapter Nine but suffice to say that how we respond to our emotions and how effectively we can stay calm during challenging or stressful situations will determine how we recover and regain composure and control. This composure allows us to apply techniques that keep us in a constructive mindset.

Composure has a bearing on how others respond around us. We have all been in a situation where someone in a leadership role has poorly reacted to a stressful situation. It flavoured everyone else's response and action as well.

A dear friend of mine, Guy, was a school principal and ran as many as fourteen schools at a time in the Northern Territory of Australia. He had to fly between his schools (to give you an idea of the scale of his role). Guy had a wonderful way of dealing with people who over-reacted and responded less than optimally when adversity and stress reared their head.

People would come to him in a heightened state, bringing a situation or a problem (rarely a solution) and wanting to know how he intended to deal with the issue.

Here was his standard answer. 'Well, do you want my reaction, or do you want my response? If it is my reaction, you can have that now, but I cannot guarantee it will be helpful or valuable. And it will likely change when I have gathered all the information I need to make a decision. If you want my response, you can have that at the end of the day / close of the week / in an hour.' (Or whatever timeline he needed to gather what he needed.)

Guy exercised a level of composure that settled everyone around him and calmed the situation. But equally importantly, he established a boundary around not being pushed into a decision he wasn't comfortable making without having all the facts. He removed any unrealistic expectations that might force a hasty decision and controlled the timeline around when a response would be given. That meant he could take control of a situation and others' emotional responses.

As we'll explore in the emotional intelligence chapter (nine), our ability to name, acknowledge or label the emotions we feel allows us to corral them, use them and distance ourselves from them when we need to.

We need to have enough self-awareness to notice how we respond and apply techniques to keep a constructive mindset. With this control, we can turn stressful situations into welcome challenges. This takes practice as we naturally have a negative bias that can cause us to react negatively.

Our brain's emotional system is designed so that negative events have a more substantial effect on us than positive or even neutral events. (This is why people will fume over the one bad social media response and miss the hundred positive ones.) In the same way, we can be affected by office gossip rather than hearing positive feedback. Ultimately, this negativity bias response can cause us to feel overwhelmed or to resist change, which will stifle a positive response to adversity. It is a matter of survival as that is where the danger lurks.

Questions to ask yourself in this area of resilience are:

Can I control my emotions, or do they control me?

Can I control my emotions, or do they control me? Do I get angry quickly and lose control? Is my emotional response in line with the reality of the situation, or am I lying in a foetal position, screaming because I can't find my car keys?

Can I identify and name my emotions? Can I sit with them? Can I just breathe through the problem?

Reasoning

The fourth facet of resilience is our level of reasoning. It's like keeping an eye on the horizon, anticipating traffic up ahead, and being ready for the idiot driver or the kid running into the road.

Reasoning plays a significant role in our confidence in our ability to creatively solve unexpected problems and adapt to sudden change. It includes our ability to be resourceful, think critically, identify opportunities and take action. Or at least adopt an action-based approach to best work towards our personal goals and/or team-shared goals.

It's not about intelligence or being the sharpest person in the room or team. That helps, but isn't a prerequisite. Reasoning is about our willingness to tackle a challenge, learn and improve, and be able to think our way through a stressful or unexpected event. It builds over time and, like any resilience domain, the more we face it, the better we get, just like learning to swim or speaking in public.

We learn to relax into an adverse situation, focus on the task at hand (not our emotional response), and act strategically.

There are many types of reasoning skills relative to the work we do. For example, lawyers and detectives need reasoning skills to take nothing for granted and question everything, even challenging their own positions.

A scientist needs reasoning skills to think critically, adopt procedures for running experiments that leave nothing to chance and have perspective skills to weed out biases.

Some argue that intuition or gut feeling is our most accurate reasoning barometer. That sixth sense, or flash of insight, is telling us something. But it may mean we abandon the act of reasoning because it feels right or is steeped in memory or experience from the past. And that may trigger our old friend, the ANS, or fight and flight response.

That feeling in your gut is the biome registering distress.

> *That feeling in your gut is the biome registering distress.*

We may then wonder about the difference between that gut feeling or intuition and anxiety. Gut feelings are related to a thing or event, whereas anxiety can be more difficult to pin down. Also, gut feelings go when a decision is made, while anxiety will hang around for far longer.

In *Nudge: Improving Decisions about Health, Wealth, and Happiness*, Nobel prize-winning economist Richard Thaler collaborated with a legal expert, Cass Sunstein. They argue that our automatic system often overpowers our reflective system, causing us to make mistakes because we go with our gut. Instead, Thaler and Sunstein feel we should purposefully engage in reflective thinking to make better decisions and design our choices in advance.[5]

Which is right?

I can't answer that. You'll have to trust your gut on that one.

Some questions to ask about your reasoning skills might be:

Can I solve problems quickly and easily? Or do I get paralysed trying to figure them out?

Do I get stuck in making decisions? Can I break down a problem into its parts and, with some methodology, determine what I can influence and what is out of my control? Can I determine the consequences of action or inaction?

Tenacity

Tenacity is about staying optimistic, responding positively, and persevering through difficulty to get back on track quickly. That's like waiting in traffic without experiencing the frustration that makes us lane-hop.

Most success in life is due to consistency rather than talent or skill. I think it was Woody Allen who once said eighty per cent of success is showing up, no matter what. If that is true, then the remaining twenty per cent of success is staying with the problem and not walking away when we feel challenged.

Being consistent often involves repetition and discipline and developing a habit of remaining with a problem longer than feels comfortable sometimes. As Albert Einstein famously said, 'It's not that I'm so smart, it is just that I stay with problems longer'.

Therefore, like reasoning, tenacity is more important than intelligence in achieving success. We don't have to be the smartest person in the room. Success comes through being more patient, regulating frustration, and focusing on the task at hand rather than the emotion it generates.

It doesn't mean we need to become immersed or wallow in the problem, but the longer we stay with it, the better our chance of figuring out the best approach.

I am sometimes asked about the difference between persistence and tenacity. As they are closely linked, they can be difficult to separate. I suggest that tenacity is a quality of determination, and persistence is about continuing on a course of action despite difficulty or opposition.

To my mind, it is a bit like an athlete training to be better at their performance. Their tenacity allows them to be more persistent in their training — to stick with it for longer to see the improvements.

Tenacity allows them to be more persistent.

Seth Rogan says 'Persistence is doing something repeatedly until it works.'[6] It sounds like 'pestering' for a reason. Tenacity is using new data to make new decisions to find new pathways to find new ways to achieve a goal when the old ways didn't work.

Telemarketers are persistent, Nike is tenacious.

Another question that sometimes arises is the difference between tenacity and stubbornness. Stubbornness is about clinging to what you know, while being tenacious is about steadily moving forward. I think stubbornness should be avoided as it suggests sticking with a problem even when we know it is useless to do so.

Tenacity is closely tied to, and essential for, reaching our goals and following our vision.

So, how can we improve our levels of tenacity? Set clear goals, ensure they align with your personal and shared vision, learn from mistakes, find opportunity (it will be there) and reject settling for less.

If we approach the situation with this level of determination, we will succeed.

I'll end with a quote from the great aviator Amelia Earhart, who said, 'The most difficult thing is the decision to act; the rest is merely tenacity.'[7]

The simple questions to ask yourself around tenacity are: Do I finish what I started? Do I stick with it? Or do I give up early?

Collaboration

The final domain of resilience I teach about is possibly one of the most critical. Collaboration is like abiding by the rules of the road and cooperating in traffic, not charging ahead without care for anyone else.

I know this book is about developing self-care, self-awareness and self-compassion, but in doing so, we have also discussed the primal human need to connect and belong to a tribe, beyond the self.

> *What we can do together is something else.*

Collaboration is the human instinct to create close connections. These provide valuable support and fulfil basic needs as social creatures. Doing something together demonstrates our collective value to secure an outcome. It's knowing that the sum will be greater than the parts, and each of our inputs is valued. Like a musician in an orchestra or band, going solo is fine but what we can do together is something else.

Collaboration involves letting others know about our shared goals. Our goals are far more achievable if we have a sense of commitment and accountability. When others know our goals and vision, a strong sense of connection and collaboration allows us all to keep focused.

Collaboration opens up a deep wealth of resources and information, which can be useful when we're reasoning or being tenacious with our problems and challenges. A collaborative experience helps us solve issues sooner, but it requires us to ask for help when we need it. That is what being part of a team is all about.

Collaboration requires strong support networks. A sense of humour is valuable as it helps us manage perceptions, supports a willingness to help others, and encourages a willingness to ask for help from others.

Acting as a mentor to other people in our group is rewarding for both parties that enjoy the connection.

True and meaningful collaboration requires four particular conditions.

1. Freedom to share information with colleagues or others in our group or community. This involves two-way feedback

between people (and leaders in a work environment). I could fill another chapter on the value of feedback, but that is for another book. In essence, feedback needs to be constructive, genuine, supportive and helpful; otherwise, it is just dumping and will get the response it deserves.

2. Psychological safety or a sense of trust. We need to know we won't be judged harshly for our input and that it is safe to have a differing opinion in pursuing a solution.
3. Opportunities to weigh in on decisions being made. This is the primary value of collaboration.
4. Solid and safe connections with others.

The best leaders can create this atmosphere and environment of collaboration, where everyone feels heard and seen. From it comes innovative solutions and engaged teams where their best work is seen.

Many of us have experienced the 'my way or the highway' leader. They made all the decisions, and we were expected to toe the line and get on with it. They were destined to fail — every time.

In high school, I played on a volleyball team. When I say 'team', I mean we gathered with a coach after school hours once or twice a week to train and play. It was a typical after-school sports scenario.

When an inter-school volleyball competition was announced, and our school was to compete, the principal chose a team of the best players across all the various sports in the school. Basically, he recruited the cream of all the talent.

I cannot remember the result of the competition, but they had no training or strategy, so I can't imagine it went well. I do know that the after-school volleyball program collapsed the following week and disappeared. How could it not? We were never even considered for the competition.

Any sense of school pride or team camaraderie dissipated, and with that went the desire to collaborate and persevere in training. In hindsight, it may have been a good call by the principal as we were absolute shit as a volleyball team! He must have snuck in to watch us play before making his decision.... Nevertheless, to not even be considered, much less have an opportunity to be part of something bigger, was the direct cause of everyone giving up.

So, as I recall that scenario, I invite you to answer the following question about your sense of collaboration.

Do the criteria for authentic and meaningful collaboration exist for you?

While this book is about self-care and wellbeing, it is also about upping your game, improving your confidence, and being centred, positive and happy, with momentum to achieve your goals through living a fulfilled and thriving life.

Wellbeing is what we seek; resilience is how we get there.

Wellbeing is what we seek; resilience is how we get there.

CHAPTER SIX

Get Out in Front

> **Questions:** Do I only react or respond when I am going off the rails? Am I aware of what will begin to slip first? Do I even know when this is starting to happen?

In this chapter, we'll look at a concept that arose from a conversation with my friend and mentor, Dan Collins. Dan represented Australia at four Olympic Games and won medals at two. He rightfully wears the title of Olympic Champion.

Dan was explaining the concept of *prehab* training, which was new to me. While I understood rehab training as recovering from injury, Dan explained that prehab training is what athletes take on before a season or an event. It involves exercising and training the parts they suspect may come under the greatest stress. Prehab training in sports follows a close process for maximum effectiveness.

> Predicting where the weak or susceptible areas are.
>
> Creating a plan to develop and improve the area.

Protecting it while we work on it, developing and strengthening the overall process.

Measuring and following ongoing progress.

Delivering outstanding performance.

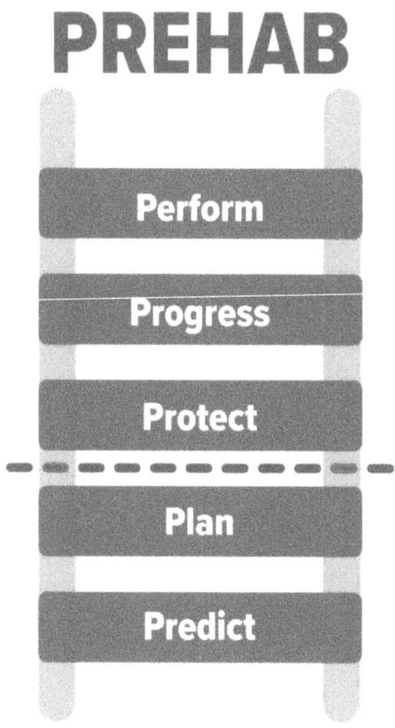

Figure 9: Prehab process

We can learn a great deal from looking at how athletes and others approach their peak performance levels. Elite athletes and sports people train in those areas that offer them an advantage (sprinters will train specifically to sprint, and swimmers also to swim faster). And they also focus on those body parts that may succumb to injury and let them down if they don't. Prehab training is about doing all we can to prevent this from occurring.

Consider the team player who continually reviews previous performances, scans the actions of the opposition to second-guess their strategy, and is ready to take advantage of any opportunity that arises. This is a mindset version of prehab training.

It involves being ready for the unseen levels of stress that those areas of the body might face. And there is excellent value in this lesson. I think mental health prehab training is an essential companion to resilience development for ourselves and indeed forms a large part of self-care.

Prehab training is like being prepared for the unexpected. For example, as explained earlier, you go to the gym and do ten squats and ten push-ups. Sure, your body is under a certain level of stress, and that is what you're resisting in doing those exercises. But it doesn't prepare you for when you might need to do twenty squats or twenty push-ups. Dan was talking about preparing parts of us to be ready to face challenges that we are yet to understand or encounter.

The concept of being 'anti-fragile' became popular about a decade ago when Nassim Nicholas Taleb published his book, *Antifragile: Things That Gain from Disorder*.[1] Taleb posits that some things seem to improve when placed in situations of unpredictability and volatile environments.

Antifragility became a kind of resilience 2.0, but whatever name we use, it generally amounts to the same thing.

> *'We can live the life we want, if we are willing to put in the work.'*

My work in resilience is influenced by the research of Jurie Rossouw, Mark McGuinness and others from the field of positive psychology. They describe resilience as being able to respond positively to adversity or challenging situations.

Mark McGuinness wrote in his book *Resilience*, 'We can live the life we want, if we are willing to put in the work.'[2]

All it takes is resilience, that ability to keep moving forward even when your inner voice is trying to prevent you from doing so.

So, in many respects, antifragility and resilience are identical to mental prehab and being mentally prepared for the unknown.

That is where mindset comes in, that set of beliefs that shape how we see the world and our place in it.

Our mindset shapes our reality. But remember, are you looking at your world through 'What's right?' or 'What's wrong?' Do you tend to focus on your strengths or on your (I hate to call them weaknesses) growth opportunities?

The positive psychology school of thought promotes leaning on strengths to continue to propel us forward. I liken this to buoyancy and the idea of rising with the tide rather than being dragged under.

This positive approach focuses attention on what is important, increases self-awareness, provides insight into what makes us distinctive, and identifies where we can improve.

Neither approach of what's wrong or what's right is exclusively correct. As with most things in life, we can take what is useful and apply that. (As long as we are not procrastinating or avoiding uncomfortable stuff.) In that way, we know we are applying part science and part art to becoming the best version of ourselves and striving for sustainable high performance.

Again, I stress that attention to the fundamentals of sleep, diet and exercise is of utmost importance. Accordingly, our mindset, mental health, resilience and attitude are necessary for sustainable high performance and a winning mindset.

It is no longer enough to target just one area in the hope that this will lift all areas of our game. We need to pay attention to all areas of our performance and mindset.

> *It is no longer enough to target just one area.*

Four main elements require our attention and focus, as reflected in this model. I have adopted this model from a quote by Stephen Covey in his work on leaving a legacy.[3]

> 'There are certain things that are fundamental to human fulfilment. The essence of these needs is captured in the phrase; to live, to love, to learn and to leave a legacy. The need to live is our physical need for such things as food, clothing, shelter, economic wellbeing, and health. The need to love is our social need to relate to other people, to belong, to love and be loved. The need to learn is our mental need to develop and grow. And the need to leave a legacy is our spiritual need to have a sense of meaning, purpose, personal congruence, and contribution'.

Let's unpack each of Covey's four elements and look at what the intersections between them could mean. The outcomes represent the value or profit from each element as they interact with one another in the pursuit of wellbeing and sustainable high performance.

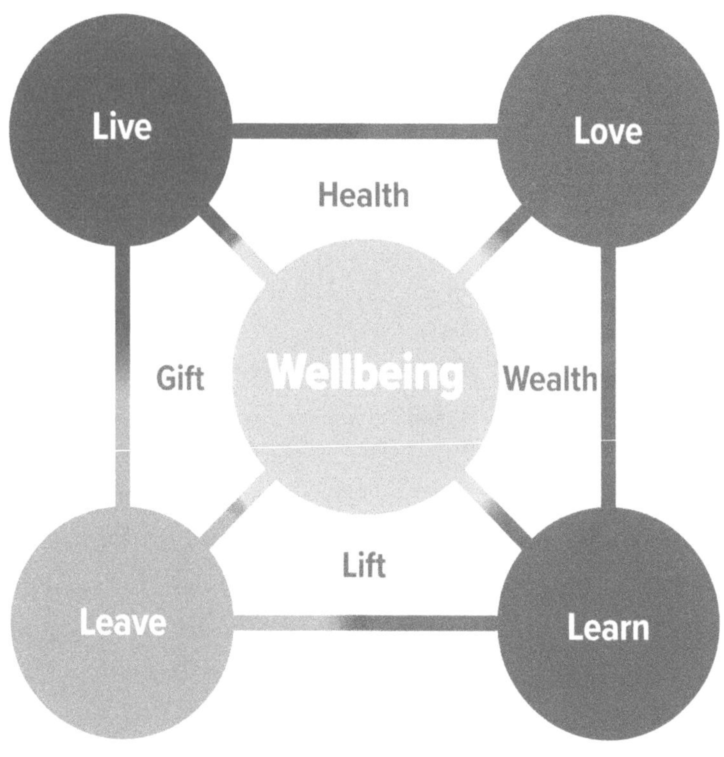

Figure 10: Living life to the fullest (based on Covey)

Live

In addition to Covey's fundamental needs to live (food, clothing, shelter, economic wellbeing and health) and our conversation earlier in this book on the need for a healthy focus on sleep, diet in all forms and exercise, we can always take an inventory of our lives.

What is working for us, and what isn't? What could be better? What could we sacrifice for more of what we want?

What does it really mean to live? We could fill a whole other book around this, but the difference between being alive and living, regularly comes up in psychotherapy.

I recall being asked, 'What do you want?' I know now that our instant response is rarely what we truly want.

A few years ago, I worked with a client who was an Uber driver. He took on the driving job out of fear of loneliness and isolation. He was shy, quiet and somewhat introverted, yet he was capable of some very insightful and deep self-exploration when the opportunity arose.

I asked him, 'What do you want?' to see where his response would go. Without going into details, he decided to explore this question with his Uber passengers, where appropriate. It was a bit risky in that some passengers may not warm to the question, and he may have come across as a bit weird. But, as he said, they would soon be out of his life, and it could start some interesting conversations or encourage people to think. The question enabled him to open conversations with strangers, which really helped his isolation and introversion.

So, what do you want from life? No, what do you *really* want from your life? Being alive is a gift, and being truly alive is to be present.

> *What do you want from life?*

Love

Love speaks to relationships, connection with others, our sense of belonging, and our primal need for safety and trust. Abraham Maslow is best known for his work on the hierarchy of needs. He wrote that the need for safety, belonging, love relations and respect can only be satisfied by other people.[4] By which he means that we cannot go it alone. As much as this book relates to self-care, we absolutely need 'other' care in our lives.

> *Do more than belong; participate.*

But genuine connection and a true sense of belonging require more than association or being with others. The American writer William Arthur Ward, said, 'Do more than belong; participate. Do more than care; help. Do more than believe; practice'.[5] We need to contribute to our tribe, to give more than receive, because this practice makes us greater than the sum of our parts. But do so in the spirit of connection and belonging.

An essential aspect of connection and safely relating to others lies in the concept of healthy boundaries, or what we often refer to as non-negotiables. We'll examine this concept in greater detail in Chapter Eleven.

Figure 10 shows that the interaction between Live and Love is Health. Without health, it stands to reason that we cannot hope to elevate ourselves to sustainable high performance.

Learn

Learn refers to our need to develop and grow, according to Covey. I also see this as our search for meaning, purpose, vision, motivation and growth. It is one of the primary facets of mental prehab. As Marshall Goldsmith wrote in his best-selling book, *What Got You Here, Won't Get You There*[6], we must continually strive to improve, learn and have our sights on where we want to go.

Having an eye on our vision allows us clear direction. Sharing this vision with others gives both collaboration and accountability. It also creates space to clarify our boundaries. And in doing so, we can grow, become motivated to pursue our vision, and continually learn as we go.

In the figure 10 model, the intersection of Love and Learn is Wealth. Far from just material wealth, it means abundance in progress, growth and performance. The old saying goes, 'Health is wealth', and it certainly rings true here.

Leave

Leave speaks to our desire to leave a legacy, to know we leave an imprint or footprint behind us, where people can gain from the lessons of our actions. An old adage says the true meaning of life is to plant trees under whose shade you do not expect to sit.

Psychoanalyst Erik Erikson wrote that as we grow older, we develop a 'concern for establishing and guiding the next generation'.[7] It's a concept he termed *generativity*: the propensity and willingness to engage in acts that promote the wellbeing of younger generations. It is the art of leaving your mark.

> *The art of leaving your mark.*

Research indicates that generativity is a strong predictor of subjective wellbeing in midlife adults.[8] But it doesn't stop there. We can see the positive effects in general mental health, agency and autonomy, connection and belonging to our groups and interpersonal relationships, and satisfaction with life and work.

So, we do not have to wait until we approach mid to later life. We can inspire and mentor those around us far earlier, particularly if we can support them as leaders in our workplaces or communities. There is a sense of generosity in spirit from helping others to achieve their, if not greatness, then at least equilibrium and satisfaction. It is a noble thing. And it is equally as valuable to us in our quest for sustainable peak performance.

We lift others through mentoring, observing and imitating. This refers to the intersection of Learn and Leave in our model. We lift ourselves and those around us to achieve our dreams and goals and raise our awareness and capability to perform at our peak as entrepreneurs. Doing so is our gift to ourselves and those within our sphere of influence.

In short, when we are at our peak in physical health and enjoy deep connection and belonging, we can consider ourselves healthy.

When we use this sense of connection to support our vision to grow. We are wealthy — not necessarily financially but on a potentially more meaningful, spiritual level. When we use our best selves to grow and achieve all we can be and do, we often organically support those around us. We are now performing at our peak levels in our business and beyond: we are engaged, empathetic and energised. We are looking through 'What's right' spectacles that shape our mindset.

Our mindset shapes our perception, which becomes our reality.

Our mindset shapes our perception, which becomes our reality. It is up to us to give ourselves the best fighting chance to seize the opportunities that come our way. And we need to be match fit to be ready for it.

CHAPTER SEVEN

Develop an Attitude of Gratitude

Questions: Do I ever stop to think about what I have rather than what I want? Do I take stuff for granted?

Gratitude is vital when working with people in recovery from an addictive process, especially in a treatment facility. One of the first things we focus on is creating a habit of looking around and within for those things for which we can be grateful.

However, there is a caveat to this. There's a danger of toxic gratitude, which means forcing someone to explore gratitude when they genuinely do not feel it. Emotions are signals or messages, and we must not shoot the messenger. We are better served by listening to the message than by overriding it with a false sense of gratitude, so pick your time for this. It is my experience that most people are ready to try this exercise. If you are not, I advocate exploring that with a primary health carer, such as your GP or a psychologist.

Evidence supports gratitude

Many books and programs extol the virtue and purpose of expressing gratitude and feeling appreciative and thankful. It is gaining plenty of attention in various fields of psychology, including positive psychology, as it forms part of a mindful reflection and focuses on the here-and-now, which, let's face it, is where everything lives and belongs.

Accumulating research is showing us that gratitude is foundational for wellbeing, self-compassion, self-care and mental health in general across our lives. Recent research has shown us that we can even measure levels of gratitude. Emmons, Froh and Rose wrote:

> 'From childhood to old age, a wide array of psychological, physical, and relational benefits are associated with gratitude. Gratitude has been shown to contribute not only to an increase in happiness, health, and other desirable life outcomes but also to a decrease in negative affect and problematic functioning.'[1]

As we explored earlier, the brain cannot focus on anxious thought patterns and gratitude simultaneously, so it can be an effective way to break the loop if anxiety is your thing. Anxiety is usually about the past or present (worry or rumination), so the antidote is to focus on the present with perspective and gratitude.

Gratitude is closely linked to optimism and resilience. It is about noticing positive elements in our lives, while resilience is finding opportunity in adversity, and optimism involves anticipating positive aspects and outcomes. They fit nicely together.

Keep a Gratitude Journal

One of the most effective ways to develop gratitude skills is to keep a gratitude journal. If this sounds a bit bloody woo-woo, I get it, but stay with me!

I think everyone should keep a gratitude journal, and I will tell you why. But first, here's how to do it.

Forget everything you've heard or read about naming five people or six things you are thankful for in your day. That is too much to concentrate on and can seem overwhelming when our minds are racing.

Instead, I suggest you find *one thing* in your day you feel grateful for. It can be a person or a thing, but you just need to name one, that is all. This is the process I always use.

> *Find one thing in your day you feel grateful for.*

Write it down somewhere. I like to use the notes app on my phone to keep track of them. That is the value in developing the habit, because here's the kicker. *You cannot name that thing or person again in the coming days.*

It's easy for the first few days. It is simple enough to express gratitude for your family, partner, job, friends, the fact that you can walk, have enough to eat, and a myriad of other assets or blessings, or whatever you like to call them.

It gets a bit harder after a few days.

Don't get me wrong. I am not saying we should no longer feel gratitude for things in our lives after we have named them. Of course, we should.

But, as we discussed in the chapter on resilience, this exercise is about developing the ability to look for the positives. It's about looking at the world through our 'What's right' spectacles rather than our 'What's wrong' spectacles.

Commit to keeping a gratitude journal for two or three weeks, and you will notice something exceptional. It will transform your outlook on life, how you relate and connect with others, and how you perceive your life. Watch how you start to seek out and see the positives in your life.

You'll develop a practice of seeing and looking for the good in your world. It becomes an automatic response to seek out what brings you comfort, peace, joy and even playfulness. You will appreciate what you have and who you have.

This exercise in self-compassion may be enough as it is, and that is fine. But if you want to, you could dig a little deeper and share your thoughts with a significant other, the kids, or someone else.

Or you can take your thoughts and journal them to a deeper level.

> Today I am grateful for ...
>
> What could have been better ...
>
> My part in what occurred (good or bad) ...
>
> The person I am grateful for today is ... because ...
>
> The best part of my day was ...
>
> To repeat that experience again, I can ...

Gratitude really works

If further conclusive proof is needed, the following is a list of twenty things that can be improved in your life by doing this exercise. Read it through, then try the exercise. Return to the list and tick off what you have noticed has improved. (If you didn't do the journal, I hope this list will motivate you to try it.)

Being aware of what you are grateful for:

1. Lowers your stress levels.
2. Induces a sense of calm. Especially if you journal at night.
3. Increases perspective and allows you to see the bigger picture.
4. Increases clarity of your situation or surroundings.
5. Improves your focus on what is important.
6. Helps you become more self-aware.
7. Becomes an excellent reference for when you are feeling down.
8. Improves mindfulness and being in the moment.
9. Helps you see the small stuff and how you relate to it.
10. Helps you recognise the good patterns and people in your life.
11. Makes you feel more accomplished.
12. Develops your empathy for others.
13. Offers a sense of motivation toward compassion.
14. Improves your inter-relational connectedness.
15. Helps you express gratitude to others.

16. Improves your levels of anxiety (you can't be anxious and grateful at the same time).
17. Relieves depression in some people.
18. Increases life satisfaction.
19. Improves your ability to see the positives in a situation.
20. Makes you a far nicer companion.

This list is by no means exhaustive, and I invite you to see if you can come up with more. Please find a way to share them with me. My contact details are at the back of the book.

Tips for journalling

Here are a few tips to help with your journalling, thanks to input from The Greater Good in Action people at Berkeley University.[2]

> Be specific. If you are grateful for someone in your life, say precisely why. Don't just mention them. That is where the magic lies. Being grateful seems to carry more weight and impact than material things. I don't really know why; it just does. Is that scientific enough?
>
> If you feel you owe someone a debt of gratitude, you may have a reason or feel compelled to thank them. Nothing wrong with that, and who wouldn't want to hear it?
>
> Go deep on why this thing or person is on your list today. That is why we say *only one thing*; it is far better than a long list.
>
> If you are struggling with coming up with something or someone for today, try shifting your mindset to what it would

be like *not* to have someone or something in your life. Don't take for granted something you would be poorer without.

Maybe focus on something that was a surprise or unintentional.

Here is a little 'Get Out of Jail' card for when you cannot think of a new thing today. Use something or someone you have mentioned in your journal previously if you can come up with a different reason to be grateful.

And, finally, if you cannot come up with anything, don't see it as a failing or a lack. Instead, read some of your past inclusions and bask in the glory and value of all that.

A gratitude attitude will change your life. Try it for a few weeks.

A gratitude attitude will change your life.

And then, commit to another two weeks! Or take a break and kickstart it again when you feel you are losing your gratitude attitude.

CHAPTER EIGHT

Gimme a Break

'You don't want to beat yourself up for beating yourself up'

— Kristin Neff PhD

Questions: Do I have a sense of self-compassion? Is it greater than my compassion for others? Does my inner voice drown out my compassion for myself? Does it feel more like self-pity?

Even though we've dipped into self-compassion throughout the book, I want to go deeper here.

The fact that you picked up this book suggests that you have some level of self-compassion. You want to understand how to improve your self-care and self-awareness levels, which requires compassion for yourself and your circumstances.

In the clinical room, I often meet with people who cannot forgive themselves or feel inadequate or undeserving of forgiveness (never mind permission to feel better). The common factors are extreme blame, shame, stigma and vulnerability. It is only when these feelings are overwhelming and manifestly interfering in their lives that they seek some help or support. Even then, shifting that mindset is challenging, requiring patience and care. There are many psychotherapy modalities with varying approaches to self-compassion, with Acceptance and Commitment Therapy (ACT) and Gestalt therapy being my preferred strategies.

Interestingly, we often hide what is happening for, or to, us, as we fear being judged or stigmatised in some way. Yet, as we are about to discover, the best minds in the field of self-compassion say that the first thing to understand and appreciate is that we all share this experience, this common humanity, and so we are not alone.

Let's look at the definition of self-compassion from the leading expert, Dr Kristin Neff. She says that self-compassion involves acting the same way to yourself when you are having a difficult time as you would to a friend. Having compassion for yourself is not very different from having compassion for others. To show compassion for another, we need to recognise and understand their feelings.[1]

Compassion means to 'suffer with'.

Compassion means to 'suffer with'.

According to Neff and her colleagues, self-compassion has three main elements.

Self-kindness versus self-judgement

Self-compassion means to be caring and understanding toward ourselves when we suffer, fail, or feel less-than. Self-compassionate people recognise that being imperfect and experiencing challenges is inevitable, so we learn to be gentle with ourselves when confronted with painful experiences. We try not to get angry at finding ourselves in this situation.

Common humanity versus isolation

Feeling irked or frustrated when things aren't as we want is often accompanied by an irrational sense of 'why me?'. Self-compassion recognises that we are not alone.

Everyone experiences and suffers from hardship. Being human means we are mortal, vulnerable and imperfect. We recognise this is something that we all go through rather than something that happens to just me.

> *Self-compassion recognises that we are not alone.*

Mindfulness versus over-identifying

Mindfulness is a non-judgemental space in which we simply observe our thoughts and feelings without trying to suppress or deny them. We can't ignore or refute a painful experience and feel compassion for it at the same time.

It takes practice, but we can learn to notice negative thoughts and feelings without taking action to avoid them.

Go back and reread Chapter Three and the sections on cognitive fusion and de-fusion to remember how we can separate from intrusive thoughts. Mindfulness is fascinating, and it's a wonderful experience to be in the here-and-now, wholly present and noticing what is, without trying to change anything.

> *Mindfulness can be practised anywhere.*

Mindfulness can be practised anywhere. When you're washing a cup in the kitchen sink, slowly and methodically notice the feel of the warm water, and focus on the soap bubbles popping. Walk very slowly on grass, with bare feet. What sensations do you feel as the grass moves between your toes?

When doing yoga or a one-minute plank, notice your thoughts and bodily sensations. A favourite practice of mine is to eat silently, or sip wine with my eyes closed. Note how taste expands when you remove sight from the equation. It's an incredible experience.

If you plan to increase your levels of meditation, then mindfulness will go a long way toward supporting your practice. In much the same way, we understand that emotions are never right or wrong; they are merely a message or a signal of what is happening. And we don't shoot the messenger.

To reach a compassionate place, we need empathy, which is an ingrained, felt sense. It's the ability to 'walk a mile' in someone's shoes, even when that takes some imagination as their experience doesn't align with ours. Compassion then expresses a desire, a thought process, that requires logic and reasoning (the pre-frontal cortex) to determine a plan and movement towards action.

If we can do that for someone else, why do we pull back from compassion for ourselves when the going gets rough? A few myths around this are well explained by Kristin Neff. The concept of self-compassion can stir up emotional responses in any of us. Some will believe that they are undeserving of it. Some will feel it is giving up to allow ourselves to feel any kind of compassion — particularly for ourselves. In other words, they think self-compassion is selfish. I am happy to report that Neff and her colleagues firmly rebut this concept.[2]

Neff offers an excellent description of what self-compassion is not. She explains the central myths of self-compassion as having a basis in other 'self' terms that have taken on negative connotations, with terms such as self-pity, self-centred, self-indulgent, self-absorbed and even selfish.

We seem to have developed this idea that:

Self-compassion is a form of self-pity and, therefore, a bad thing. Except that it is really the antidote to self-pity. It allows us to be more willing to accept and experience difficult feelings with some kindness. When things are going wrong for us, we can see this as a part of life that everybody experiences from time to time.

Self-compassion means weakness. Studies show that self-compassion is a potent source of coping and resilience.

Self-compassion is a potent source of coping and resilience.

Self-compassion is narcissistic. This opens a conversation around the difference between self-esteem and self-compassion. Although both are related to psychological wellbeing, self-esteem is often an evaluation or measure of some kind (feeling better than others) and can fluctuate wildly depending on circumstances. Self-compassion doesn't measure or judge at all. It says we all share imperfections.

Self-compassion is selfish. The idea of caring for the welfare of others often comes with the idea that we must treat ourselves poorly. This isn't an either/or scenario. Neff says, 'The irony is that being good to yourself actually helps you be good to others. While being bad to yourself only gets in the way.'

Self-compassion makes us complacent. Once again, the research tells us that self-compassion is far more effective as a force for personal motivation than self-recrimination or self-punishment. Far from evading personal responsibility, it strengthens it.

We have spoken about empathy and emotional intelligence. Frankly, having compassion for yourself is no different than having compassion for others. However, you don't always get 'two for the price of one', so we will explore that shortly.

To have compassion for others, you must experience or notice their suffering. This is empathy. The word compassion means to *suffer with*. You may feel moved by their experience, and you respond with a desire and a move to help in some way. To experience this means that we accept that suffering, imperfection, failure, shame and vulnerability are all part of the shared human experience.

Why do we find it so difficult to exercise compassion and forgiveness for ourselves if we can feel it for others? Why do we hold ourselves to a different standard? Is it a fear of self-indulgence or self-pity? Are we afraid to accept our weaknesses or frailties, in case they overwhelm us?

It is perfectly okay to forgive ourselves in the moment. When working with people overcoming an addictive process, where they may have behaved in ways that paralyse them with shame and guilt, it is common to say, 'That is something you did, it is not who you are'.

We need to increase our self-compassion for self-care and self-awareness. Self-compassion is linked in the research to reductions in mental and physical health issues like anxiety, depression, physical pain and overload of the stress hormone cortisol. On the flip side, it has also been shown to improve and increase motivation and mindset and enhance wellbeing in general.

We seem able to have far greater empathy for others than we feel for ourselves.

In the third part of this book, Looking Out, we'll explore the concept of emotional intelligence and consider empathy's role in it. In her 2011 research, Ashley Mae Skoda found that self-compassion was correlated with forgiveness. Specifically, the positive aspects of self-compassion, like mindfulness and self-kindness, were closely related to the forgiveness of others.[3]

Kristin Neff devised a self-compassion test, which she has freely shared with the world. It covers all aspects of self-compassion, including self-kindness, self-judgement, common humanity, isolation and mindfulness. If you want to complete the test and find out your score, follow this link. https://self-compassion.org/self-compassion-test/

You will have noticed that previous chapters included questions to explore your personal experience of the concepts discussed. In this chapter, I leave it to Neff's test. How do you self-score on the following? A simple yes or no will give you a result.

> I'm disapproving and judgemental about my own flaws and inadequacies.
>
> When I'm feeling down, I tend to obsess and fixate on everything that's wrong.
>
> When things are going badly for me, I see the difficulties as part of life that everyone goes through.

Thinking about my inadequacies tends to make me feel more separate and cut off from the rest of the world.

I try to be loving towards myself when I'm feeling emotional pain.

When I fail at something important to me, I become consumed by feelings of inadequacy.

When I'm down and out, I remind myself that many other people in the world feel like I am.

When times are really difficult, I tend to be tough on myself.

When something upsets me, I try to keep my emotions in balance.

When I feel inadequate in some way, I try to remind myself that feelings of inadequacy are shared by most people.

I'm intolerant and impatient towards those aspects of my personality I don't like.

When I'm going through a very hard time, I give myself the caring and tenderness I need.

When I'm feeling down, I tend to feel like most other people are probably happier than I am.

When something painful happens, I try to take a balanced view of the situation.

I try to see my failings as part of the human condition.

When I see aspects of myself that I don't like, I get down on myself.

When I fail at something important to me, I try to keep things in perspective.

When I'm really struggling, I tend to feel like other people must be having an easier time of it.

I'm kind to myself when I'm experiencing suffering.

When something upsets me, I get carried away with my feelings.

I can be a bit cold-hearted towards myself when I'm experiencing suffering.

When I'm feeling down, I try to approach my feelings with curiosity and openness.

I'm tolerant of my own flaws and inadequacies.

When something painful happens, I tend to blow the incident out of proportion.

When I fail at something that's important to me, I tend to feel alone in my failure.

I try to be understanding and patient towards those aspects of my personality I don't like.

If this subject is new to you, I hope it helps raise your awareness of self and the idea that we are all in this shitshow together. It is okay not to be okay, and you can cut yourself some slack. What a wonderful world it would be if everyone could do this in a healthy way.

Cut yourself some slack.

PART THREE

LOOK OUT

CHAPTER NINE

See Me, Know Me: See You, Grow You

Questions: Can I take my emotional experience and use it to see others? Can I see how my emotional responses can influence other people? Can I use this for good?

Our entire approach to radically upping our self-care requires us to be aware of what fires us up and makes us angry, what calms us down, what excites us, what brings us joy, and what brings up feelings of shame and embarrassment (which can lead to us feeling stigmatised or judged).

Like most men, I've often shied away from asking for help when I needed it — especially if the support is for something society thinks I *should* be able to do. Such reluctance amongst men to seek help for traditionally masculine tasks is so common that there are countless memes and pop-culture references. The quintessential examples include asking for directions, lifting something heavy and changing a tyre.

When I lived in Ireland, the AA (Automobile Association) was a roadside vehicle-recovery service. On the rare occasion when I asked for help, I had no choice. I was caught in the rain on the side of a highway with a flat tyre, but without the correct tools to change it. I struck up a conversation with the AA guy who came to my rescue and asked if they were all mechanics. He told me that they weren't. Not everyone needed to be a mechanic, but they all knew enough to get a car started or towed.

Fast-forward many years later to Australia, where I found myself in a similar predicament. I called the NRMA (National Roads and Motorists' Association) as the car I was driving was missing a jack. The representative arrived, and I immediately felt a withering glare from him. I was a young, strong and fit lad, and he clearly judged me as more than capable of changing a tyre. Or, at the very least, he thought I should have had the common sense to keep a jack in the car!

He went to work, and, in the strained atmosphere, I tried to strike up a conversation with him — much like my enjoyable conversation years earlier in Ireland. I asked, 'Are the NRMA guys all mechanics?' Without looking up or pausing, he sneered, 'No. We're all f@*king pastry chefs!'

I can laugh about it now, but I still recall the emotions of being belittled, judged and made to feel 'less than'. It was enough to make me retreat from the conversation and seek the safety of the driver's seat. I needed help and didn't have the tools, so I reached out for help and was scorned for it.

> *If you feel it, then it is real.*

I didn't know what to name it at the time, but I would have felt stigmatised. Or self-stigmatised. And that is the thing about stigma. Whether or not it is just your perception, if you feel it, then it is real. Sometimes the distinction is defined by stigma and self-stigma (the internalised shame you put on yourself).

Stigma is often invisible. Discrimination is a close cousin of stigma and is more visible, which is why we have laws that protect the vulnerable. Discrimination does, but stigma sees.

That is the thing about emotions. There traditionally exists a stigma related to showing our emotions. Growing up, we heard adults telling us to get over it, or don't cry, or pull ourselves together. We were made to feel bad for feeling bad. Or worse, we were berated, belittled or judged for doing so, known as emotional invalidation.

We learned self-awareness was self-indulgent, while self-compassion was deemed self-pity and, therefore, a bad thing.

Self-awareness is the ability to acknowledge, recognise, own and understand what makes us tick. These are our values, emotional needs, strengths and weaknesses. And they are the first step on the journey of emotional intelligence.

I raise this point to make several others.

Emotions make our experiences exciting, vibrant and fulfilling. Emotions play a defining role in how we think, behave and relate to others. They forge our responses to our environment and can influence the emotions of others around us. They affect our behaviours (go shopping when you're hungry, you will see what I mean!).

We can experience mixed emotions; in other words, we can swing between conflicting emotions rapidly. But usually, one is louder and making itself known, swapping places in our awareness.

Emotions are simply a message. Don't shoot the messenger. Emotions are neither right nor wrong; they are merely a barometer for what we are experiencing. We need to feel *all* our feelings. We too often suppress, avoid, deny, or ignore them. Or we simply do not have the capacity to identify them, name them, or sit with them.

> *Emotions are simply a message.*

Developing this skill is the crux of emotional intelligence.

Emotional intelligence (EQ) protects us from burnout and the self-stigma (and the resulting anxiety) we can experience.

Rubén Trigueros and his colleagues published research into the role of emotional intelligence in self-stigma and burnout. They found that self-stigma is positively related to burnout syndrome. Thus, the findings indicate that emotional intelligence may have a protective role against self-stigma, which is closely related to burnout syndrome.[1]

Emotional intelligence offers us the capacity for empathy. If you are looking for inspiration to increase your level of emotional intelligence and empathy, be aware that Travis Bradberry and Jean Greaves called emotional intelligence 'the single biggest predictor of success in the workplace'. They calculated that people with high EQ made an average of US$29,000 more annually than those with lesser EQ. It was related to their ability to interact with others, experience empathy and compassion and read the room. Bradberry and Greaves believed high EQ made better leaders.[2]

The following model shows the journey of emotional intelligence skills.

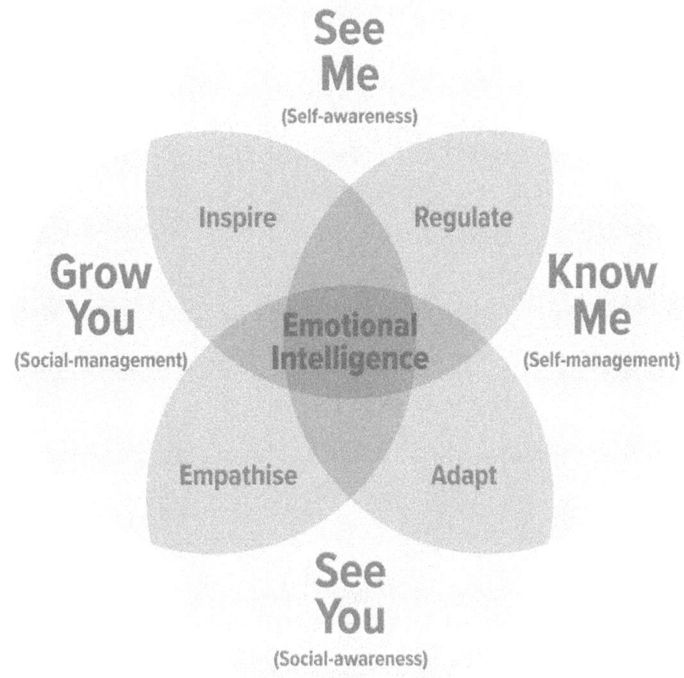

Figure 11: Elements of emotional intelligence

> *The EQ journey begins with self-awareness.*

The EQ journey begins with self-awareness, which isn't easy for many people because of how they were raised or their experience of seeing emotions rejected, ignored, or suppressed. There can be a lot to unlearn. This is usually the foundational work for clinical therapy, supporting someone to learn to experience themselves fully, to be able to name and sit with their emotional response.

When we master this, we learn that emotions are cues or messages. They usually form our actions and responses. So, we pay attention and try to figure out what they mean. Once we can do that, we can learn to manage them. Rather than being overwhelmed by our feelings, we use them effectively, respond in healthy ways and learn to regulate rather than repress our emotions.

The next stage is to adapt our regulation skills to better spot others' emotional responses. Not just to see how our emotions affect others, but how theirs can influence us.

Being able to see another's perspective is a valuable gift. This other, or social, awareness is the first step towards empathy. In the words of the philosopher Henry David Thoreau, 'Could a greater miracle take place than for us to look through each other's eyes for an instant?'

That is what Bradberry and Greaves meant when they claimed emotional intelligence as the single biggest predictor of success. It is the ability to read the room, understand what motivates others, and create the right atmosphere for meaningful engagement.

I believe the two most important facets are self-awareness and empathy.

We experience emotions at every moment. They influence our decisions whether we realise it or not. We may not always be aware of the emotion as they often last mere moments, except for sadness, which seems to last up to 240 times longer than any other emotion, according to Philippe Verduyn and Saskia Lavrijsen.[3]

I used to think that we experience emotion, at some level, from the moment we wake up to the time we go to sleep. But, of course, we also experience emotions when we sleep (think dreams and nightmares). And there is no doubt that sleep quality affects emotions.

So, it makes sense that we want to master our ability to become aware of and regulate our emotions and feelings constantly.

Increasing self-awareness and recognising emotional responses is not difficult, but it takes time to master the skills. Try these steps.

Notice how your emotions make you react and respond to your environment. What comes up for you? Is it a reasonable response?

Notice how they make others respond.

Learn to name your emotions.

Learn to sit with them. Ask yourself, 'what is this I am feeling right now? What is happening to make it noticeable? Does it make sense to me? What do I want to do with this feeling? Am I okay to sit with it for a minute? Is there a better way for me to respond?'

Remember that emotions are neither right nor wrong — they just are. They are a messenger. Don't invalidate them. Remember what happened when you were young and made to feel bad for expressing your emotions?

Emotions are neither right nor wrong.

Cut yourself some slack. Maybe take a breath if you need to. A big one.

Take time out if you need to. Just remember, you are doing this to regulate, not to avoid the feeling or emotion. You are just preparing to deal with something in a better way when you feel ready.

It is okay not to be okay.

Different levels of empathy

Recently, I have been working across Australia with leaders, groups and teams involved in responding to Covid (in the health sector) and floods and natural disasters (local government and health sectors). Empathy raises its head as a topic all the time. Are we displaying empathy? Do we have enough empathy? Are we capable of empathy, or are we jaded?

I've noticed that leaders' responses are relative to the level of compassion fatigue they are experiencing. Or the level of vicarious trauma or survivor guilt their people are experiencing. We can definitely become overwhelmed by it all.

> *Our response to others' plight depends on our emotional intelligence.*

Ultimately, though, our response to others' plight depends on our emotional intelligence.

Leaders can also have a different experience, depending on how far removed they are from ground zero. This is so in any environment, not just in health or local government.

What are your leaders' levels of compassion like? Are they exhausted from trying to keep this shitshow together? Are they naturally empathetic? Are they worn out?

Contemporary research looks at three kinds of empathy.[4]

Cognitive: noticing the effects on their people, not always driven to respond.

Emotional: often impulsive desire to understand and resonate.

Compassionate: driven by a deliberate desire to help.

The research breaks down even further into sympathy vs empathy vs compassion. It all gets a bit confusing, but we'll leave that for another conversation.

It may help to view empathy as a continuum or scale. At the lower end, we might see sympathy for the plight of others. Sympathy is basically feeling sorry for someone.

Recent research with patients in a palliative care facility demonstrated their aversion to sympathy and pity. It didn't resonate at all and even had a negative effect on their experience.

In the middle, we see empathy and a desire to understand their experience better.

Both these processes are instinctive and don't require a frontal cortex thought process. We feel them viscerally and mirror what we are seeing. It's an emotional response, much as we cry during a movie or watching a horrific news story on television.

Often, we then have a thought process where we are driven or strive to action or to act compassionately towards others.

We want to support or help. This isn't completely instinctive as it involves processing the event thoughtfully and deciding on a response.

You now have a clear understanding about empathy and compassion and where they come from. So, let me ask you this. Can you see a relationship between compassion and self-compassion? Because despite how you answer that question, it has been reasonable to assume that someone who is compassionate will also have a high level of compassion for themselves.

But recent research implies that self-compassionate people are not always compassionate to others. They don't seem to be related. López, Sanderman, Ranchor and Schroevers found that most people tended to feel more compassion for others than themselves.[5] Compassion may have evolved more for social wellbeing, while self-compassion (which targets self-judgement) has a more significant direct impact on personal wellbeing. From an evolutionary perspective, compassion in partners meant a greater chance for survival.

That makes sense when we view burnout in leaders who work hard to ensure their team's psychological safety but hold themselves to a higher or different standard and give themselves a hard time, feeling they 'should' be able to cope. That was certainly my personal experience as a leader, and I see it continually in my work with leaders and burnout.

Bummer! That means we have more work to do to develop both areas of compassion, as we need to tackle them differently.

Let's look at self-compassion. It is an essential skill if we are to exercise healthy emotional regulation and mastery. We will need to learn to quieten the self-critic, our internal monologue that beats us up for the slightest grievance.

To increase our self-care levels, we need to see when the going is tough and acknowledge it. Our self-care should be steeped in compassion rather than treated as a chore to be completed.

When we struggle against the odds for a while, we need to learn to be kind to ourselves rather than judge ourselves for being unable to keep up. After all, everyone has a breaking point, every lightbulb will fail, and every hard drive will eventually fail. With enough stress and overload, for long enough, everybody succumbs.

So, when we appreciate that everyone can become a member of our burnout club and we are all in this together, just with different membership levels, that shared or common humanity can allow us some self-compassion.

This goes a long way to not over-identifying where we may find ourselves.

As discussed in Chapter Eight, Kristin Neff is highly accomplished in this field. Seek out her work, as it is excellent at framing and supporting self-compassion. In short, Neff says that with self-compassion, we give ourselves the same kindness and care we'd give to a good friend.

Isn't it the case that our self-critic will speak to us in a way that we would never speak to anyone else? Whoever said we had to be perfect (except ourselves)? And how can we be compassionate to others and not give ourselves the same levels of care?

According to Neff, there are three main areas of self-compassion. If we can get these messages across to ourselves, we can live a different life and dramatically lift our self-awareness and compassion for ourselves and others.

> *It is okay not to be okay.*

First, it is okay not to be okay. Rather than getting frustrated and angry when life falls short of ideal, we can learn to accept that these difficulties are inevitable. Cut ourselves some slack and say, 'This is shit, but it could happen to anyone. Today I will feel sorry for myself, but tomorrow I will deal with it and move on.'

Second, we are all in this together. 'Why does this always/only happen to me? Firstly, it doesn't only happen to me; it could happen to anyone. And in fact, it often does. Today, it is just my turn.'

And third, don't make it any bigger than it needs to be. Self-compassion allows us to take a balanced approach and sit with the feelings and emotions that are stirred up. Remember, feelings and emotions are merely signals for what is going on for us. Don't shoot the messenger. Instead, see them with some openness and clarity for the experience rather than judge ourselves for it.

Here are some useful exercises for developing self-compassion.

If this happened to a friend, what would you say to them? It will likely be very different to what you say to yourself. Change what you are saying to be more friendly, and speak to yourself in the third person, if that helps. You can reframe your inner dialogue when you notice you are being a little tough on yourself.

Trust me; you are not alone in that. Everybody has things they don't like about themselves. Things that make them feel shame, insecure or not good enough. Write that shit down. Keep a journal to help process the challenging parts of your day.

Learn to write compassionately, as this will lift your self-kindness and common humanity skills.

Write a private letter to yourself from a place of acceptance and compassion. Maybe you can tell your car dashboard all about it! Or see a therapist to help you make sense of it.

Ask for a hug if you can. If you can't, you may be surprised to learn that you can hug yourself and get the same result. We can activate the parasympathetic nervous system simply by using supportive touch, so a gentle arm rub or deep self-hug will work wonders. Try it.

You can hug yourself and get the same result.

When we have a good handle on self-compassion, we can increase resilience skills as we begin to see opportunity in adversity.

The difference between an event and the memory of it

Here is an interesting fact about emotional responses and reality. They don't have to happen at the same time. For example, we don't have to be in an argument to experience emotions and feelings. Our emotional response can be revisited when we are ready to deal with something. How often have you revisited an argument in your mind and wished you had said something different?

We don't have to be eating our favourite meal; we only need to imagine we are, and our stomach juices will flow and our mouths start to water.

It is the same with sexual fantasy. The brain doesn't need to know the difference between an event and the memory of it to experience the emotional effects.

We can use this to our advantage as we explore our self-awareness safely and often. In my work as a Gestalt therapist, we use a process known as the Empty Chair experiment.

This simple approach allows you to work through interpersonal or internal conflict or express and process grief or anger. It helps you see the situation differently and gain insight into your feelings and behaviours.

This is how it works:

You sit facing an empty chair. In the chair, you imagine a person with whom you need to relate. Then, you speak to the empty chair. You explain your feelings, thoughts, and understanding of the situation.

Now things get really interesting. After you've shared your side of things, you move to the other chair. Then you respond to what you just said from that person's perspective. In a way, you are taking on their role. You may move back and forth between the chairs several times to continue the dialogue.

I understand if that all sounds a bit woo-woo (and most clients need time to adjust to the idea before commencing the work). But what becomes apparent is the importance of saying what you need to say. Working through the emotion and gaining perspective is vastly more important than having the other person hear it.

It means you can finish an argument safely or work through the grief of missing someone and not saying goodbye, which is far better than dwelling on an unresolved emotional response.

Having solid and comfortable control and mastery of our emotions allows us to explore empathy.

We are born with a natural level of empathy.

I believe we are born with a natural level of empathy. It is a fundamental skill to belong, communicate, and relate to others. Frans de Waal, a Dutch primatologist and ethologist, believes it's both nature and nurture.[6] He says that empathy is innate — inherited through genes — but also that a person can learn to become more or less empathetic.

Other research points to a more profound understanding of how particular brain activity becomes prominent when we are in pain and see others in the same situation.[7,8]

Similarly, there's growing research on mirror neurons and how we react to seeing someone else's struggle. This is a reciprocal and equal brain cell response when we perform an action and witness someone else perform the same action.

Instead of our brains using logical thought processes to interpret and predict other people's actions, we understand others by feeling. Mirror neurons allow us to make sense of other people's intentions and actions and interpret facial expressions. It is now thought that mirror neurons are the neurological basis of empathy.[9] The old saying, 'I feel your pain' makes sense, doesn't it?

It also makes sense that we can improve our empathy muscles. Try talking to new people. At the core of empathy is curiosity, so start a conversation with someone you don't know well or even a stranger. Get past the small talk.

I recall travelling with an Uber driver (not the one I worked with as a client) who softened the conversation by asking for contributions to a 'passenger playlist' he was creating. He wanted a classical and a contemporary song. I gave him my ideas. (I don't know what program or app he was using, but he was able to add them to his collection through voice command/prompt.)

After he insisted that we loudly sing the song together, I told him the 'What do you want' story. He said he has wonderful, deep conversations with fascinating passengers, and would adopt this question as an opener. He then asked me, 'What do you want?' (Asking a psychotherapist that question is bound to get a detailed answer.) We are rarely asked what we want, so I hope the opportunity is refreshing for his passengers, and the practice gives him some valuable perspectives.

CHAPTER TEN

We've Got Yer Back

At the age of six, I had to get spectacles to see properly at school. I felt the full brunt of teasing and name-calling, with the usual 'four eyes' name-calling and the like. My glasses defined me as different from the other kids. In the grand scheme of things, it was no big deal. It wasn't malicious bullying, just insensitive teasing.

But I remember that it stung and continued until the teacher heard a couple of classmates teasing me. He rounded on them solidly to make sure it never happened again. I can still recall that warm feeling of safety and belonging I experienced from being validated, protected and supported by the teacher.

Now, imagine feeling judged or stigmatised about having reading glasses in the office and unable to let anybody know we needed to wear them. What sort of a challenge would that be? The level of mental health challenges in the workplace is roughly the same as the number of people who wear reading glasses, by some measures, so it makes for a good analogy.

This chapter explores how to look out for each other in a safe and supportive way. Belonging to our 'tribe' is hugely important in our

Belonging to our 'tribe' is hugely important.

journey through self-awareness, compassion and care. Knowing how to look out for each other and developing our empathy and communication skills are essential to keeping us safe.

We will examine what to look for, what to say when we see something and how to support someone who needs to know that it is okay not to be okay.

The main point I want to stress here is that *we don't need to rescue or save anyone*. We are not counsellors, social workers, therapists, psychologists or psychotherapists (well, I am...), and only we need to have our own answers. We are far better off asking how we can support someone than telling them what they should do to get better.

There is a wealth of information and research on the common factors that support someone recovering from mental health issues.[1,2] All the research boils down to the idea that community support (family, friends, workplace) and a sense of hope for the possibility of recovery represent about seventy per cent of the likelihood of getting better.

Leave the advice to people who know these things.

Create space for belonging and safety in your team. It is okay not to be okay.

In Chapter Two on burnout, I made the point that we are more likely to spot the signs of burnout in someone else before we see them in ourselves. I need to clarify that we may see the symptoms and signs in ourselves, but because we hold ourselves to be different, with high standards, we don't allow ourselves or permit ourselves to be less than our best.

> *Create space for belonging and safety in your team.*

Do you find yourself thinking, 'I should be able to deal with this!' Or perhaps 'I should be taking this in my stride; look how the others are managing'. Maybe your inner voice is saying, 'Come on! Get your shit together, you've got this!'

That was certainly my experience. I was very mindful of my team and did all I could to clear the path so they could function at their best. But I gave myself a hard time for not coping.

Our internal monologues can be very cruel. (I use this term loosely because some people experience visualisations rather than hear a voice. But I am referring to how we communicate with ourselves.) I have heard it said that we have more conversations with ourselves than all other conversations combined. And because of our natural negative bias, which is a survival instinct, we pay more attention to adverse events. These self or inner conversations tend to be self-doubting, self-reproachful and self-critical.

In his book, *The Voices Within*, Charles Fernyhough suggests that our inner voice runs at an average pace of 4,000 words per minute – ten times faster than verbal speech.[3] We don't even have to use complete sentences when talking to ourselves because we know exactly what we mean. Throw thoughts steeped in anxiety into that mix and see what you get.

So, it is very likely that our self-critical voice gets a lot of attention, and when we feel we are somehow disconnecting or not keeping up, we give ourselves a hard time.

> *Sometimes self-care isn't enough.*

But, when we see something happening in another, we can be very forgiving in comparison. In her book, *Burnout: The Secret to Unlocking the Stress Cycle*, Emily Nagoski says that sometimes self-care isn't enough, and we need to rely on others around us.[4]

They say it takes a village to raise a child. Not literally in this case, but to ensure everyone in your team is looking out for each other, sharing a vision and responsibilities, and cooperating.

In Chapter Two, we also discussed how the level of apathy or cynicism could tend to spread through a team. If someone feels that way, they will want to ensure they don't struggle alone and try to recruit others to their 'side'. This is a normal human response to needing to belong and remain connected. This mindset can be contagious if allowed to continue unchecked.

But the conversation is rarely around feeling vulnerable or struggling with self. It will always be someone else's fault. We externalise the issue as victims of circumstance or another person's problem.

If you have ever lived with or been part of the world of someone in an addictive process, you will have seen this play out in an exaggerated form. Relapse resulted from something happening *to* them at someone else's hand. They reckon they are never at fault; they are victims of circumstance. This is rarely malice or deception at play; it is purely a survival instinct. When the brain cannot deal with a situation or issue that is too big to contemplate, the result can be denial.

It will be the same with someone experiencing apathy or cynicism in the workplace. They will seek out allies and support within the team to assure themselves that they are not alone and validate what is happening to them. It isn't nasty — at least it doesn't usually start that way.

Another related survival instinct that arises when someone feels like this is the idea of stigma.

Even the definitions of stigma in the literature, particularly when discussing mental health, see stigma as 'the disgrace, social disapproval, or social discrediting of individuals with a mental health problem'. Or stigma refers to the discrediting, devaluing and shaming of a person because of their characteristics or attributes. I'm sure you will agree this is terrible language.

And it doesn't matter whether someone is actually experiencing this level of judgement or whether we just perceive it may occur. We keep the perception (real or imagined) to ourselves for fear that we will be seen as 'less-than'. Not team players, not up to the task, unreliable or the weakest link in the chain.

So, let's take a look at how to approach this scenario.

Remember, we are not out to rescue or save anyone. We just want to let them know they are safe and supported.

That is all. If we can do that effectively, then we have done a very good thing.

What to look for

Spotting when a team member is struggling with a mental health challenge is a paramount skill, especially for a people leader.

I don't necessarily mean just managers, although they certainly fit the bill, but anyone in a team who has gained the respect of their peers. That probably means you. I reckon if you are reading this book, you already have some level of self-awareness and empathy.

When a team captain leads their team onto the pitch, they must be able to spot when someone is starting to limp or faces a challenge in playing their best. The captain needs to know how it will affect the player and the team's performance.

Given that one in four of your work team will experience a mental health issue this year, you, as team captain, can expect that more than one person will be affected.

The captain must deal with the issue, support the player in getting the right rehab and recovery and readjust the team strategy.

The captain is never the physio or injury expert. The captain doesn't need to know or advise what anyone should do to get better.

Unless the captain has first-hand experience with the same injury, any advice they offer at this point will be useless to the player.

It begins with being able to spot the challenge.

We use an acronym, PAGER, to highlight the different areas for clues about how someone is coping. (For anyone under thirty, a pager was a pre-smartphone device that alerted you to an incoming message. If you were super-cool (like me), you clipped it on your belt so everyone could see you were important! Oh, dear....)

Anyway, PAGER in this context refers to Performance, Appearance, Growth, Emotions and Relationships. Let's look at each.

Performance

Despite best efforts, our ability to perform at our best is challenged — even in roles we are passionate about. Performance is lower than expected or normal. Impaired ability is frustrating when someone loses the capacity to recall names and do basic maths or needs to read emails five times before the information sinks in.

Appearance

This can be tricky, especially if the person works remotely for some or all the time. We can still notice changes in behaviour, such as leaving their camera off, low energy or vitality in their posture, and personal care and hygiene taking a back seat.

Growth

Someone burnt out may lose sight of the team's shared vision and purpose, self-purpose or self-motivation has slipped, and they may express a loss of hope. Gordon Parker and his colleagues describe this as dealing with a candle that has blown out instead of one that is fading.[5] Similarly, our response to someone losing this shared purpose and someone who has lost it will be different.

Emotions

Emotional regulation is a valuable asset but is not always within reach of someone struggling to be at their best — especially if their self-critic has a loud voice. In working with people recovering from an addictive process, anger, irritable outbursts, and even rage are often the only emotions left. In its wide-ranging spectrum, anger tends to reveal itself most readily.

Nothing upsets group equilibrium like emotional outbursts from someone not behaving normally.

Relationships

Isolation and loneliness are hugely damaging.

Relationship problems manifest as people isolating, becoming withdrawn, not speaking up in meetings, and not connecting in a supportive and healthy manner. Unhealthy boundaries harm the relationships necessary for good teamwork. Isolation and loneliness are hugely damaging.

What to say

Words matter. And most people fear speaking to someone who might be struggling. What if I say the wrong thing? What if I am the problem? They seem so irritable lately that I don't want to set them off. What if I do reach out, and they become a burden on me? (Spoiler alert — this is a myth. It never happens).

The opposite is the well-meaning but clumsy person, who wants to help and takes on the role of the white knight with all the answers.

I recently had a bout of pneumonia and lost count of the number of well-meaning but annoying saviours who told me to take vitamin C to clear it. It is the same with advising someone struggling with mental health issues.

We have no idea of their journey, their issues, what they are doing to recover or how they are coping.

If I were to get a tattoo, I think it would be these words: Ask, don't tell.

Ask, don't tell.

There is a reason why every psychiatrist, psychologist, psychotherapist, counsellor, social worker and couples counsellor uses what we call 'I' statements or 'I feel' statements.

A gentle inquiry that begins with concern for the other person will be far better received than unsolicited advice. We are hard-wired to experience concern. It generates a dopamine response in both parties that just feels good.

The opposite of this — something beginning with 'You ...' is far more likely to get anyone's defences up. (If you ever want to start a fight with someone, just rattle off three sentences beginning with 'You should'... and it will be all on.)

So try, 'I am concerned that you may be struggling' or perhaps 'I am a little worried about you', or maybe 'I've noticed you aren't your usual bubbly self and felt I wanted to check in with you'.

These will be far better received than 'What's up with you? or even 'You've been a bit quiet lately'. Or, worst of all, 'What have you got to be anxious/depressed about?'

Of course, picking your moment to check in with someone can also hugely affect the response you will get. I am sure you will appreciate that this is not a spectator sport. We don't need witnesses.

Choose somewhere private and quiet — not as you're coming out of a meeting. Put away your phone. Take a seat beside them rather than across an office desk (a table in a café or canteen is fine as it is neutral).

Try not to sound like you are reading from a script.

It is perfectly fine to say if you feel a little nervous.

I wish all of this were obvious, but it really isn't and needs to be said. I have experienced the aftermath of lousy timing, not being discreet, reciting some kind of script, and the 'tough love' approach (a devastatingly poor idea).

> *Nobody expects you to have the answers.*

A few things to remember: The responsibility for accepting or getting help and support rests with them. All you are doing is creating some safety for them to feel it. *You are not a counsellor.* Nobody expects you to have the answers (except maybe yourself, and you'd be wrong).

Oh, and one further thing: I'd like to dispel any notion that the other person will become a burden on you. It doesn't happen — especially if you aren't trying to rescue or save them. You are empowering them to take the steps they need to. You are offering choice and safety. And that is all.

However, *they* may feel they can't say anything in case they become a burden. Both parties might feel this could happen, but it doesn't. Instead, you both will experience an oxytocin and dopamine response from the interaction. It's a lovely, warm, connecting experience. If it feels weird or uncomfortable, just say so, smile together and continue.

We can do a lot to create that environment for those around us. And we don't have to be experts in anything.

What will we do

That brings us to the next part of the interaction.

If you get a negative response (and that's likely the first time you approach someone), remember, their heightened sense of anxiety, shame or stigma may viscerally prevent them from opening up to you.

In this instance, I say something like, 'Okay, good to hear it. I just thought I would check in with you because I felt concerned. I will probably check in again with you in a week or so, but in the meantime, if you do want to chat or anything, you know where I am/have my number, so reach out to me.' They may deflect your concern and say they are fine, thanks.

Please don't get into a whole thing. Remember, you were only creating a safe space for them, so don't make it unsafe for you. If you get a bullish response, it is okay to say, 'No problem, I was just a little concerned. Only a friend would ask.'

You may get a positive response, and they say something like, 'Yeah, I am struggling at the moment, thanks for noticing'.

Or, 'I don't know what to do, and I can't think straight anymore'.

Our standard answer is 'Okay, how might we ...'.

Now, we can get into how you can support them to feel seen, valued, heard, safe and belong.

'Okay, sorry to hear that. How might we help you in this?'

'How might I support you?'

'What would help you right now?'

'If you felt I/we could help somehow, what might that look like?'

'Is there something we can do here at work to help?'

They may say that two weeks in Fiji should do the trick. I would usually respond with, 'Yeah, and I'd like a thirty-inch waist, but neither of these will happen! But would you like me to accompany you to see your boss about some support?' or perhaps 'Can I help you get an appointment with your GP?' Or, 'Do you want to go for a walk and a chat?'

Empower them to make the decision.

Whatever you do to help, empower them to make the decision. It is their journey, after all. The 'How might we...' approach empowers them in the solution and opens up the possibility of trying something different with some support.

It also connects you as someone trusting and safe. And both of you win in that scenario.

What are the most important messages in all of this? *Ask, don't tell …* and *How might we ….*

Think about the others in your team right now. Are you concerned about someone? Do you feel you can approach them? What might be stopping you?

CHAPTER ELEVEN

Where My Shit Ends and Yours Begins

*'Balance is not better time management,
but better boundary management.
Balance means making choices
and enjoying those choices.'*
— Betsy Jacobson

Questions: Do I know what my boundaries are? Are they absolutely non-negotiable? Do I keep them to myself or tell others?

This chapter looks at some of the activities, behaviours and processes we use in relationships and how we connect with others.

Boundaries keep us safe

At one point, I worked in a clinical addiction treatment facility with a young man with chronic substance use problems. This young lad had been so deep in his addiction for so long that he'd pretty much lost his sense of self.

One day when in our care, he was getting a haircut. He made a comment to the hairdresser, and she felt aggrieved enough to make a complaint. Of course, such events are dealt with swiftly and severely in a treatment centre. He was summarily dealt with as he didn't offer anything by way of defence.

Sometime later, his side of the story finally came out in therapy. I could see how his comment could have been misconstrued. But when I asked why he hadn't said anything at the time, he responded, 'Shit like this has happened to me my whole life', (which was true as well). He had lost so much of his sense of self and value that he felt he probably deserved what he got. He no longer had a boundary around his self-worth.

> *We need to know we can trust the people we work with.*

We learn the value and importance of relationships, feeling safe, and feeling like we belong with other people. Not just within our families or communities but in our workplaces. It is fundamental, primal. We need to know we can trust the people we work with. An integral part of self-care is ensuring our relationships are helpful and healthy and that we are connecting in a wholesome way.

But, an essential element of looking out for ourselves involves boundaries. You may know them as non-negotiables or priorities.

For example, take a moment and check if you have a boundary around switching off from work at the end of the day. If so, that's great. If not, I strongly encourage you to develop one. And that would be one of your non-negotiables.

This is particularly relevant to people working in remote or hybrid environments, who have yet to develop healthy patterns of bookending the day to switch between work and home or family life.

An essential aspect of connection and safely relating to others lies in the concept of healthy boundaries, or what we often refer to as non-negotiables. I am not a great fan of the word 'non-negotiable' because I don't believe anything is so entirely fixed. That would be a barrier, not a boundary. It could be as unhelpful and unhealthy as having no boundary at all because it prevents dialogue, discourse, or negotiation. It breaks connection.

But by all means, if non-negotiable allows you to clarify what you need to prioritise, then use it as an internal conversation. However, you may need to negotiate with yourself if your boundaries are ever crossed. For example, I have a boundary (a non-negotiable) around exercise. Nothing should get in my way and prevent me from getting to the gym. Everyone I work with knows this. But work sometimes gets in the way, and I need to compromise. At that point, I negotiate with myself to ensure I can fit my exercise in somewhere else. But it does happen.

We'll go into the differences between each of these shortly. But, suffice to say, even though 'non-negotiable' is not the best description, whatever name we give it, this is one of these most important elements of self-care.

Define your limits

As Sandra Yancey says, 'I don't manage time; I manage boundaries, and the time looks after itself', which I think is a powerful statement. It makes perfect sense. So, let's briefly explore what we mean by a boundary.

'Your boundary' is a term frequently used in psychological circles, as it is your declaration of what is okay for you and what isn't.

It's the limit we set with other people or situations. It can refer to the sense of decency and moral compass, or it can be what we feel safe around. The bottom line is that boundaries exist to protect us.

I am often asked the difference between a non-negotiable and a boundary. To me, non-negotiable sends an internal message that something is important to you. When you relate it to others, it becomes your boundary.

I also get asked about the difference between a boundary and a priority. I define a priority as a ranking rather than a behaviour, so you can prioritise your boundaries.

And then, I am asked to explain the difference between a boundary and a barrier. My boundary is the line between my priority and other people's needs. Basically, it's where my shit ends and theirs begins. At the same time, a barrier is an obstacle designed to stop anything, as stated earlier. I think a barrier is unhealthy because it breaks the connection with other people. We can hide behind a barrier. Some people also refer to barriers as their non-negotiables.

Negotiating the negotiables

In practical terms, I think everything needs to be negotiable.

For example, let's say you have a non-negotiable around ensuring you exercise every day at 5:30pm. You need the flexibility to say, 'I have a work commitment that needs to be addressed in support of the rest of my team. But it's at a time when I would normally exercise.' You could negotiate with yourself to meet the team's needs while reserving the right to ensure that you can exercise at another time.

That's negotiation. It's a healthy response to a need in your environment. It also means that we get to support the people around us while ensuring we meet our own needs.

The critical point here is that I am the one who negotiates the change to my boundary or the change to my non-negotiable. I need to ensure that I have the autonomy to control my non-negotiable. If my boundary is ruptured, we'll need to find a way to correct that.

So, what's the difference between control or manipulation and a boundary? I think control is trying to make others do or be what you want them to do or be. In contrast, a boundary makes it safe for us to be ourselves. Boundaries show the line where we hold our self-care routines.

My boundary is the line where I end, and everything else begins.

There are many instances where people cannot support themselves around a boundary. For example, in the military, you don't get to say or do what you think supports yourself. And you end up having to do something that could betray your sense of inner peace, values, or understanding of what is right. That is the equivalent of having no boundary, and that process is known as moral injury.

Moral injury, or moral distress, used to be considered a part of post-traumatic stress disorder (PTSD), but, to my mind, it's completely separate. I see this issue in many industries and sectors where in the course of doing their work, somebody feels their sense of what is right and proper is betrayed. For example, in local government, somebody may have a strong sense of what is decent and right in terms of the environment. Yet as part of their role, they need to approve a construction or roading project. It betrays their sense of right, but is in the service of their role. And that can be a moral distress.

I have heard people working in the online gambling industry say they can see the harm gambling can cause to individuals. And it betrays their sense of decency. People in the tobacco or fast-food industries can sometimes feel that too.

The Covid pandemic has raised similar issues. We need to be mindful of the sense of moral distress people have had around being vaccinated (or not) and coming back to the workplace.

Setting boundaries and sticking to them is about exercising personal choice. It teaches us that we really do control what is most important to our self-care.

When I see this contradiction over the inflexibility of non-negotiables or barriers, I visualise a shoreline where the water reaches the beach. It is constantly in motion, but there is always a point at which the water meets the sand. That is a boundary. I need to be able to see it and know where it is and whether it gets changed.

In Chapter Four, I explained that the brain is a fluid-moving organ, and our treatment or mistreatment will affect how it behaves and supports us. All of the areas of healthy brain activity are important. So, for example, we can create a boundary around sleep or taking breaks.

> *We often confuse sport, exercise and play.*

We can prioritise other areas, such as play. We often confuse sport, exercise and play. We play golf or tennis, but that is just exercise. We play video games, but they are just precursors to escaping reality and have a soothing function.

By play, I mean rolling on the floor with the kids, colouring in with them, and inventing games. I am talking about your dog's excitement when you rattle their leash or grab their ball. Maybe it's playing charades with a bunch of slightly tipsy friends and having a good belly laugh.

Have a game of tennis using your non-dominant arm, if you want to have a giggle.

Research increasingly tells us of the huge importance of play. Find those things that bring you joy. Indulge in them as often as you can. Everything depends on it.

Another critical aspect of being mindful around boundaries or non-negotiables is that they can feel like they could start an argument, friction, or conflict with other people.

What I know about boundaries

Here's what I have learned about boundaries. You'll remember some of these from earlier in the book.

The only people who will ever negatively react to your boundary are those who stand to gain by you not having one. In general, when we declare a boundary, priority, or non-negotiable, another party recognises that by saying, 'Okay, now we know their limit. We know what is important to them and will work around it or meet them halfway.'

Instead of assuming that declaring your boundary will cause friction, recognise that they reduce conflict and maintain healthy emotional energy.

Knowing boundaries exist can reduce stress levels.

Knowing boundaries exist can reduce stress levels. They improve our sense of balance and self-care and strengthen relationships and connections with other people.

You may notice that children push until they find what is (and isn't) acceptable behaviour. That's a typical example of when a declared boundary is of value. The other great advantage is that declaring your boundaries and stating what's important to you makes you more reliable and trustworthy.

My colleague and friend, Joe Hart, recently wrote that one carefully timed 'No' is worth a hundred 'Yeses'. That's because it lets others know our limits.[1]

Declaring your boundaries is not confrontational. Rather, it makes you more reliable and trustworthy while defending your rights and your needs for self-care. Nothing is more important than that.

In work environments, I often ask leadership teams whether they think their people can push back when they feel overwhelmed or have too much work. Research says that seventy-five per cent of leaders will say 'Yes, of course, their people can push back', and they are open to negotiating what the employee needs to ensure that the business needs are met. But only thirty-five per cent of employees agree that's the case.[2]

There is a huge gap between the perception of leaders and the individual's experience.

It raises interesting conversations around how we can push back if we think a boundary is being overrun. How can we say no to our boss or somebody demanding more time or energy? And are there supportive ways of saying 'No'?

At this point, I usually refer to the strategy used by comedians and improv comedy theatre. They invite the audience to suggest a scenario for the actors to perform without prior warning. The actors have no scripts, and they've had no information to prepare. And they have to come up with and keep a scenario moving for as long as possible. It is hugely entertaining to watch.

The one golden rule actors must stick to is that they never say 'No'. They can only say 'Yes-and'. That is how we can respond to somebody who asks too much of us, transgressing our boundaries, or not paying attention to where we're not negotiable.

A simple strategy plenty of people use effectively is to say something like, 'Let me look at my diary'. Or 'Let me look at my existing commitments'. Or even, 'Let me look at my priorities and then come back to you'.

These buy you time. They put you in the driving seat. The other person must wait until you've given it as much consideration as possible to determine whether you can meet their need. And if you can't, you can say so.

If your boss asks you to do something extra, the 'Yes, and...' strategy is very useful. Answer with something along the lines of, 'Yes, we can meet that priority, and I will need help from you to determine what can fall off the other end'. In other words, I will need your help to look over my growing list of things to do and determine what isn't a priority if you want me to meet this new one. If you expect me to deliver my best work across all of them, I will end up disappointing us both and not doing as good a job as we know I can deliver.

That's negotiation, and it empowers you to work with your leader to determine the new priorities without overwhelming you. You haven't said 'No', but you have negotiated your boundary.

It can sometimes help to create a list of all tasks you have to do, identify what is urgent and important, and rank them. In his seminal book, *The 7 Habits of Highly Successful People*, Stephen Covey spoke about this using a quadrant model.[3] The idea originated with US General Eisenhower and is an excellent way of determining what must get done and what can be pushed to the side or re-prioritised.

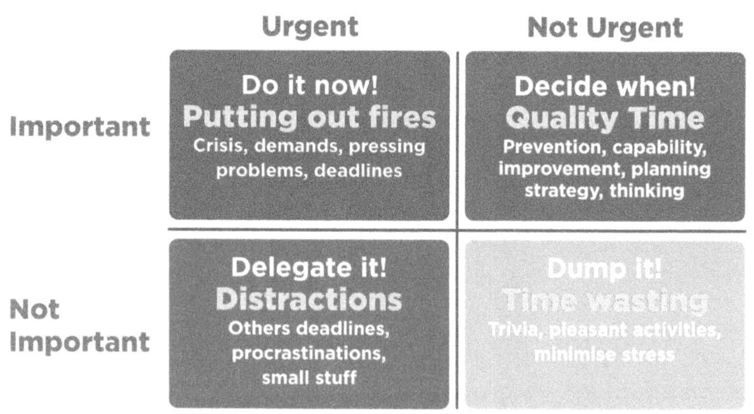

Figure 12: Urgent/Important quadrant model

Remember A well-considered 'No' is worth a hundred lazy 'Yeses'. It's a way of proving you're committed to doing your best. But it is also about how much energy you apply to your tasks. And that's what

Sandra Yancey meant when she said she manages her boundaries and the time takes care of itself.

So, at the end of this chapter, I invite you to look at your action plan. And perhaps take a look at your things to do list. If you don't have one, create one and determine what is urgent, what's important and include your non-negotiables and your boundaries in that list. They must be there so you can determine how much time you need to allocate to everything. You will be better for it, and so will the people with whom you relate and connect.

Look at your action plan.

Afterword

Well, we made it. Thank you for sticking around, and I sincerely hope you have found some insights and 'whys' for upping your self-care game to be the best you can be. Or to get back on track if that was your motivation.

As I said at the start, my aim for this book is to broaden perspectives on what we need to do to raise our self-awareness and get some clarity on where we can improve. But that is only part of the story.

Everybody experiences difficult or challenging times, and there is definitely a need for self-compassion and recognising that life isn't all sweetness and light or beer and skittles.

It is essential to know that we are not alone when this is happening to us. There is shared humanity, as Kristin Neff calls it, and we do not have to walk this lonely and challenging track alone. Life can be brutal, hard and cruel sometimes, but everyone experiences that. So, if you are, give yourself a break, allow it to happen and dust off for another day.

There is much we can do to support ourselves.

I did say that this book isn't another 'Eat your veggies and get off your arse' self-help book. The focus has been less on the 'what' or 'how' and more on the 'why'. The few times I went to the 'what' was in service of your self-care and when a concept may be new or different.

I have been around the block a few times, and this book is an accumulation of lessons I've learned and tried to instil in others to support their wellbeing. Lessons from when I was more involved in the clinical side of caring for people at the sharp end of life.

If I have learned anything, it is that we cannot just focus on the parts that seem to be suffering. There is so much we can radically do to lift ourselves, using our strengths to bolster us while dealing with what needs help.

Despite all our efforts, burnout and mental health issues like anxiety continue to rise in today's workplace. But we tend to react to problems rather than be proactive.

Mental health is so much more than an absence of illness; therefore, it is in our best interests to do all we can to lift our game and aim for sustainable performance. It improves our lives in every aspect through emotional, physical and spiritual engagement, with a sense of belonging and the ability to support each other.

What's next? Go to my website www.markbutler.com.au to download the free action plan that goes with this book.

Choose the elements of self-care highlighted throughout the book and begin your journey to sustainable performance. Commit to actions that will up your self-care to levels you may not have focused on before.

Then, keep an eye out for my next book, *Up Theirs*, coming in 2023. It's mostly for people leaders, but aren't we all leaders in some way when we motivate and support those around us? We will explore the value of looking out for each other on a deeper level. We will deepen our connection to our emotional landscape and develop empathy and compassion in the service of others.

You can find me on LinkedIn, dive into my website, and if you feel inclined, get in touch and share with me your journey of upping your self-care and gaining sustainable high performance.

I'd like that.

About the Author

Mark Butler, MAddBeh, MGestTher, CReC, MPACFA (Clin), is a clinical specialist and mental health strategist for mental health in the workplace. He has more than twenty-five years of corporate experience and fifteen years as a clinical psychotherapist and clinical director.

As a risk specialist, Mark helps individuals, teams and organisations worldwide get in front of potential mindset and mental health issues. He teaches them to deal effectively with individual and team burnout to optimise resilience, promote growth mindset and wellbeing, and create the conditions to deliver sustained peak performance.

Mark combines his clinical expertise and commercial acumen in a compassionate, personable approach that normalises the conversation around mental health, putting everyone at ease and delivering results.

A regular guest on webinars, podcasts and conferences, Mark is an international best-selling co-author, coach and mentor.

Contact Mark

mark@markbutler.com.au

www.markbutler.com.au

www.linkedin.com/in/mark-butler/

References

Introduction

1. Sinek, S. (2009). *Start With Why: How great leaders inspire everyone to take action*. London: Portfolio/Penguin.
2. Sinek, S. (2009). *How great leaders inspire action*. [online] Ted.com. Available at: https://www.ted.com/talks/simon_sinek_how_great_leaders_inspire_action?language=en

Chapter One

1. Sharma, M. (2022). '"Busy is the New Stupid" – Warren Buffet', *Education World*.
2. Billman, G.E. (2020). Homeostasis: The Underappreciated and Far Too Often Ignored Central Organizing Principle of Physiology. *Frontiers in Physiology*, [online] 11(200). doi:10.3389/fphys.2020.00200
3. Mofolo, T. (2021). *Your Diet Is Not Only What*. [online] Available at: https://themindsjournal.com/your-diet-is-not-only-what
4. Kabat-Zinn, J. (n.d.) Working With Thoughts While Meditating. https://www.masterclass.com/classes/jon-kabat-zinn-teaches-mindfulness-and-meditation/chapters/working-with-thoughts-while-meditating
5. Pilcher, J. J., Ginter, D. R., & Sadowsky, B. (1997). Sleep quality versus sleep quantity: relationships between sleep and measures of health, wellbeing and sleepiness in college students. *Journal of Psychosomatic Research*, 42(6), 583-596.

6. Jessen, N.A., Munk, A.S.F., Lundgaard, I. & Nedergaard, M. (2015). The Glymphatic System: A Beginner's Guide. *Neurochemical Research*, [online] 40(12), pp.2583–2599. doi:10.1007/s11064-015-1581-6.

7. Reeves, B.C., Karimy, J.K., Kundishora, A.J., Mestre, H., Cerci, H.M., Matouk, C., Alper, S.L., Lundgaard, I., Nedergaard, M. & Kahle, K.T. (2020). Glymphatic System Impairment in Alzheimer's Disease and Idiopathic Normal Pressure Hydrocephalus. *Trends in Molecular Medicine*, 26(3), pp.285–295. doi:10.1016/j.molmed.2019.11.008.

8. www.sclhealth.org. (n.d.). *Why It's Time to Ditch the Phone Before Bed*. [online] Available at: https://www.sclhealth.org/blog/2019/09/why-it-is-time-to-ditch-the-phone-before-bed/#:~:text=Stop%20using%20electronic%20devices%2030

9. Bigalke, J.A., Greenlund, I.M., Nicevski, J.R. & Carter, J.R. (2021). Effect of evening blue light blocking glasses on subjective and objective sleep in healthy adults: A randomized control trial. *Sleep Health*, 7(4). doi:10.1016/j.sleh.2021.02.004.

10. Texas Exes (2014). *University of Texas at Austin 2014 Commencement Address - Admiral William H. McRaven. YouTube*. Available at: https://www.youtube.com/watch?v=pxBQLFLei7O

11. Yuval Noah Harari. (2017). *Homo Deus - Yuval Noah Harari*. [online] Available at: https://www.ynharari.com/book/homo-deus/

12. Mayer, E.A. (2018). *The mind-gut connection : how the hidden conversation within our bodies impacts our mood, our choices, and our overall health*. New York Harper Wave.

13. Ferranti, E.P., Dunbar, S.B., Dunlop, A.L. & Corwin, E.J. (2014). 20 Things you Didn't Know About the Human gut Microbiome. *The*

Journal of Cardiovascular Nursing, [online] 29(6), pp.479–481. doi:10.1097/jcn.0000000000000166.

14. Johns Hopkins Medicine. (2019). *The Brain-Gut Connection.* [online] Available at: https://www.hopkinsmedicine.org/health/wellness-and-prevention/the-brain-gut-connection
15. Kabra, N. & Nadkarni, A. (2013). Prevalence of depression and anxiety in irritable bowel syndrome: A clinic based study from India. *Indian Journal of Psychiatry*, [online] 55(1), pp.77–80. doi:10.4103/0019-5545.105520.
16. Robinson, K.M. (n.d.). *What to Do When Depression and Anxiety Mix*. [online] WebMD. Available at: https://www.webmd.com/depression/features/anxiety-depression-mix#:~:text=Depression%20and%20anxiety%20are%20like [Accessed 2 Oct. 2022]
17. Wise, H. A. (2018). *A Gut Feeling: Conquer Your Sweet Tooth by Tuning Into Your Microbiome*. Rowman & Littlefield.
18. Amir, S., Brown, Z.W. & Amit, Z. (1980). The role of endorphins in stress: evidence and speculations. *Neuroscience and Biobehavioral Reviews*, [online] 4(1), pp.77–86. doi:10.1016/0149-7634(80)90027-5.
19. Rafiq, K., Adnan, B., Khalid, A., Akram, A., Saify, Z.S., Usman, T., Khan, S., Qureshi, H. & Ashraf, H. (2019). Physical Work Out: An alternative therapy for stress & depression. *FUUAST Journal of Biology*, [online] VOL. 9(NO. 2). Available at: https://fuuastjb.org/index.php/fuuastjb/article/view/418
20. Fountoulakis, C. (2019). *Heart Rate Variability Training and Control of Emotions*. Doctoral thesis. Manchester Metropolitan University.

Chapter Two

1. Moss, J. (2019). *Burnout Is About Your Workplace, Not Your People*. [online] Harvard Business Review. Available at: https://hbr.org/2019/12/burnout-is-about-your-workplace-not-your-people
2. American Medical Association. (n.d.). *WHO adds burnout to ICD-11. What it means for physicians*. [online] Available at: https://www.ama-assn.org/practice-management/physician-health/who-adds-burnout-icd-11-what-it-means-physicians#:~:text=Burnout%20appears%20in%20the%20ICD
3. Parker, G., Tavella, G. & Eyers, K. (2021). *Burnout : a guide to identifying burnout and pathways to recovery*. Crows Nest, Nsw: Allen & Unwin.
4. Lamers, F., van Oppen, P., Comijs, H. C., Smit, J. H., Spinhoven, P., van Balkom, A. J., & Penninx, B. W. (2011). Comorbidity patterns of anxiety and depressive disorders in a large cohort study: the Netherlands Study of Depression and Anxiety (NESDA). *The Journal of Clinical Psychiatry*, 72(3), 3397.
5. ibid
6. van der Kolk, B.A. (1994). The Body Keeps the Score: Memory and the Evolving Psychobiology of Posttraumatic Stress. *Harvard Review of Psychiatry*, [online] 1(5), pp.253–265. doi:10.3109/10673229409017088.

Chapter Three

1. www.drtracyphd.com. (n.d.). *Future Tense: Why Anxiety is Good For You*. [online] Available at: https://www.drtracyphd.com/future-tense

2. Carroll, L. & Ward, M. (2022). *Lockdown toll: One in eight has new mental health condition.* [online] The Sydney Morning Herald. Available at: https://www.smh.com.au/national/nsw/lockdown-toll-one-in-eight-have-new-mental-health-condition-20220513-p5al4v.html
3. Leaf, C. (2021). *Cleaning Up Your Mental Mess: 5 Simple, Scientifically Proven Steps to Reduce Anxiety, Stress, and Toxic Thinking*. Grand Rapids, MI: Baker Books.
4. van der Kolk, B.A. (1994). The Body Keeps the Score: Memory and the Evolving Psychobiology of Posttraumatic Stress. *Harvard Review of Psychiatry*, [online] 1(5), pp.253–265. doi:10.3109/10673229409017088.
5. Thich Nhat Hanh Quote Collective. https://thichnhathanhquotecollective.com/2021/04/22/6417/
6. Xanitha, Z. (n.d.). *Home*. [online] Zjamal Xanitha. Available at: https://zjamalxanitha.com

Chapter Four

1. Phelps, K. (2021). *How To Keep Your Brain Young: Preserve memory, reduce dementia risk, harness neuroplasticity and restore function*. Macmillan Australia.
2. Mail Online. (n.d.). *Pace of life speeds up as study reveals we're walking faster than ever.* [online] Available at: https://www.dailymail.co.uk/sciencetech/article-452046/Pace-life-speeds-study-reveals-walking-faster-ever.html
3. Dr. Dan Siegel. (n.d.). *Healthy Mind Platter*. [online] Available at: https://drdansiegel.com/healthy-mind-platter/

4. Brené Brown. (n.d.). Dare to Lead | True belonging never asks us to change who we are. [online] Available at: https://brenebrown.com/art/true-belonging/

5. Robinson, L. (2019). HelpGuide.org. [online] HelpGuide.org. Available at: https://www.helpguide.org/articles/mental-health/benefits-of-play-for-adults.htm

6. Rossi, E.L. (1991). The Twenty Minute Break: Reduce stress, maximize performance, improve health and emotional well-being using the new science of ultradian rhythms. Los Angeles: Tarcher.

Chapter Five

1. Rossouw, J., Rossouw, P., Paynter, C., Ward, A. & Khnana, P. (2017). Predictive 6 Factor Resilience Scale – Domains of Resilience and Their Role as Enablers of Job Satisfaction. *International Journal of Neuropsychotherapy*, 5(1), pp.25–40. doi:10.12744/ijnpt.2017.1.0025-0040.

2. Silverman, M.N. & Deuster, P.A. (2014). Biological mechanisms underlying the role of physical fitness in health and resilience. *Interface Focus*, [online] 4(5), p.20140040. doi:10.1098/rsfs.2014.0040.

3. Ballenger-Browning, K.K. & Johnson, D.C. (2010). *Key Facts on Resilience*. [online] Semantic Scholar. doi:10.1037/e717302011-001.

4. Committee on the Department of Homeland Security Workforce Resilience; Board on Health Sciences Policy; Institute of Medicine. (2013). *A Vision and Goals for Workforce Readiness and Resilience*. [online] *www.ncbi.nlm.nih.gov*. National Academies Press (US). Available at: https://www.ncbi.nlm.nih.gov/books/NBK201683/

5. Thaler, R.H. & Sunstein, C.R. (2008). *Nudge: Improving decisions about health, wealth, and happiness*, New York. N.Y: Penguin Books.

6. November 2 and 2013 (2013). *Tenacity is not the same as persistence*. [online] Seth's Blog. Available at: https://seths.blog/2013/11/tenacity-is-not-the-same-as-persistence/#:~:text=Persistence%20is%20doing%20something%20again

7. BrainyQuote. (2000). *BrainyQuote*. [online] Available at: https://www.brainyquote.com/quotes/amelia_earhart_120929

Chapter Six

1. Taleb, N. N., (2012). *Antifragile: things that gain from disorder*. New York: Random House.

2. McGuinness, M. (2012). *Resilience: Facing Down Rejection and Criticism on the Road to Success*. Ebook ed. Lateral Action Books.

3. Covey, S.R., Merrill, A.R. & Merrill, R.R. (1995). *First things first: to live, to love, to learn, to leave a legacy*. New York: Simon & Schuster.

4. Maslow, A.H. (n.d.). A Dynamic Theory of Human Motivation. In: *Understanding human motivation*. [online] pp.26–47. doi:10.1037/11305-004.

5. www.goodreads.com. (n.d.). *A quote by William Arthur Ward*. [online] Available at: https://www.goodreads.com/quotes/314867-do-more-than-belong-participate-do-more-than-care

6. Goldsmith, M. (2010). *What Got You Here Won't Get You There: How successful people become even more successful*. Profile books.
7. Erikson, E., & Erikson, J. (1981). On generativity and identity: From a conversation with Erik and Joan Erikson. *Harvard Educational Review, 51*(2), 249-269.
8. Ackerman, S., Zuroff, D.C. & Moskowitz, D.S. (2000). Generativity in Midlife and Young Adults: Links to Agency, Communion, and Subjective Well-Being. *The International Journal of Aging and Human Development*, 50(1), pp.17–41. doi:10.2190/9f51-lr6t-jhrj-2qw6.

Chapter Seven

1. Emmons, R.A., Froh, J. & Rose, R. (2019). Gratitude. *Positive psychological assessment: A handbook of models and measures (2nd ed.).*, pp.317–332. doi:10.1037/0000138-020.
2. Berkeley.edu. (2018). *Gratitude Journal (Greater Good in Action).* [online] Available at: https://ggia.berkeley.edu/practice/gratitude_journal

Chapter Eight

1. Neff, K., & Knox, M. C. (2016). Self-compassion. *Mindfulness in Positive Psychology: The science of meditation and wellbeing, 37*, 1-8.
2. Neff, K. D., & Germer, C. (2017). Self-compassion and psychological wellbeing. In E. M. Seppälä, E. Simon-Thomas, S. L. Brown, M. C. Worline, C. Daryl Cameron, & J. R. Doty (Eds.),

Oxford Handbook of Compassion Science (pp. 371–385). New York: Oxford University Press.

3. Skoda, A.M. (2011). *The Relation Between Self-Compassion, Depression, and Forgiveness of Others.* [online] etd.ohiolink.edu. Available at: http://rave.ohiolink.edu/etdc/view?acc_num=dayton1314061381

Chapter Nine

1. Trigueros, R., Navarro, N., Cangas, A.J., Mercader, I., Aguilar-Parra, J.M., González-Santos, J., González-Bernal, J.J. & Soto-Cámara, R. (2020). The Protective Role of Emotional Intelligence in Self-Stigma and Emotional Exhaustion of Family Members of People with Mental Disorders. *Sustainability*, 12(12), p.4862. doi:10.3390/su12124862.
2. Bradberry, T., & Greaves, J. (2009). *Emotional Intelligence 2.0.* TalentSmart.
3. Verduyn, P. & Lavrijsen, S. (2014). Which emotions last longest and why: The role of event importance and rumination. *Motivation and Emotion*, 39(1), pp.119–127. doi:10.1007/s11031-014-9445-y.
4. sites.google.com. (n.d.). *Empathy Training Lit Review - Cognitive Empathy.* [online] Available at: https://sites.google.com/site/empathytraininglitreview/definitions/cognitive-empathy
5. López, A., Sanderman, R., Ranchor, A.V. & Schroevers, M.J. (2017). Compassion for Others and Self-Compassion: Levels, Correlates, and Relationship with Psychological Well-being. *Mindfulness*, 9(1), pp.325–331. doi:10.1007/s12671-017-0777-z.

6. sites.bu.edu. (n.d.). *Nature vs. Nurture» the nerve blog | Boston University*. [online] Available at: https://sites.bu.edu/ombs/tag/nature-vs-nurture

7. Bu.edu. (2010). *All About Empathy» the nerve blog | Blog Archive | Boston University*. [online] Available at: https://sites.bu.edu/ombs/2010/07/24/all-about-empathy/

8. Oktem, E.O. & Cankaya, S. (2021). *Empathy for Pain*. [online] *www.intechopen.com*. IntechOpen. Available at: https://www.intechopen.com/chapters/74491

9. Thagard, P. (2007). I Feel Your Pain : Mirror Neurons, Empathy, and Moral Motivation. *Journal of Cognitive Science, 8*(2), pp.109–136. doi:10.17791/jcs.2007.8.2.109.

Chapter Ten

1. Weinberger, J., & Rasco, C. (2007). Empirically supported common factors. In S. G. Hofmann & J. Weinberger (Eds.), *The Art and Science of Psychotherapy* . Routledge/Taylor & Francis Group. pp. 103–129.

2. Leibert, T.W. & Dunne-Bryant, A. (2015). 'Do Common Factors Account for Counseling Outcome?', *Journal of Counseling & Development*, vol. 93, no. 2, pp. 225–235.

3. Oyebode, F. (2017). The Voices Within: The History and Science of How We Talk to Ourselves By Charles Fernyhough Profile Books. 2016.£ 16.99 (hb). 352 pp. ISBN 9781781252796. *The British Journal of Psychiatry, 210*(2), 170-171.

4. Nagoski, E., & Nagoski, A. (2020). *Burnout: The secret to unlocking the stress cycle*. New York: Ballantine Books.

5. Parker, G., Tavella, G., & Eyers, K. (2021). *Burnout: A guide to identifying burnout and pathways to recovery*. Routledge.

Chapter Eleven

1. Hart, J. (2022) True Perspective: Why leading with the truth always wins. Melbourne: Hambone Publishing.
2. Greenwood, K., Bapat, V. & Maughan, M. (2019, October 07). *Research: People Want Their Employers to Talk About Mental Health*, Harvard Business Review.
3. Covey, S. R. (1991). *The 7 Habits of Highly Effective People.* Provo, UT: Covey Leadership Center.

CPSIA information can be obtained
at www.ICGtesting.com
Printed in the USA
BVHW010601110223
658270BV00023BA/1194